BEYOND
THE WALLS
OF CONFLICT

Mutual Gains Negotiating for Unions and Management

BEYOND THE WALLS OF CONFLICT

Mutual Gains Negotiating for Unions and Management

DR. DAVID S. WEISS

IRWIN
Professional Publishing®
Chicago • London • Singapore

Times Mirror
Higher Education Group

Library of Congress Cataloging-in-Publication Data

Weiss, David S. (David Solomon), 1953–
   Beyond the walls of conflict : Mutual gains negotiating for unions and management / David S. Weiss.
     p.   cm.
   Includes bibliographical references and index.
   ISBN 0-7863-0795-1
   1. Collective bargaining. 2. Labor disputes. 3. Negotiation in business. 4. Dispute resolution (Law) I. Title.
   HD6971.5.W45   1996
   331.8—dc20   95–46600

Printed in the United States of America
1 2 3 4 5 6 7 8 9 0 BS 3 2 1 0 9 8 7 6

*This book is dedicated to Nora and Joseph—
who fill my world with love and meaning.*

PREFACE

Union-management wars intrigue people more than union-management peace. War captures media attention. It remains front-page news for days if not weeks. The passion to have winners and losers draws the interest of the public and receives intense attention.

Peace reaches the media on the day the negotiators sign the treaty. Afterwards, peace is not of interest to the public. The problem is solved and people find another war on which to focus.

Union-management peace is even less appealing for people who want to justify their existence and be noticed. In the political realm of union representation, membership opinion and election often determine whether someone continues to work in a leadership role or returns to the assembly line or service position. A union-management war harnesses the interest and public goodwill of the membership and demonstrates that the representative is doing something. Concessions from the company gained in the settlement almost guarantee union representative reelection.

On the management side, negotiators' careers are made and broken based on their success or lack thereof during collective bargaining. If they negotiate a good deal for the company, they often are promoted and have the blessing of never having to

negotiate a union-management agreement again. If they negotiate a bad deal, or even worse, a work stoppage, they may be
released from the company. Negotiators often hope for a winning
peace in which they can demonstrate union concessions so they
become the heroes and do not have to do archaic collective
bargaining again.

One astute union negotiator said that the only thing we
know is that the way we do it today will need to be different
tomorrow. Union-management peace is not the obvious preferred route for negotiators, but it is in the common interest of
companies and unions.

WINNING INDUSTRIAL PEACE THROUGH MUTUAL GAINS NEGOTIATING

In numerous situations, the desire for union-management peace
has finally arrived. Management and unions have a thirst for
information and techniques to apply the principles of peace in
the workplace. Works by Kochan and Osterman (1994) support
the trend that an environment in which union and management
have a peaceful relationship can outperform a nonunion work
environment.

A significant problem emerges in establishing a collaborative direction. While the desire for mutual gains negotiating is
there, no usable guide exists to instruct the negotiators about how
to proceed. Most of the works in this area are driven by academic
analysis or by conceptual presentations. Even the *Getting to . . .*
books by Roger Fisher (et al.) do not present a systematic, usable
presentation of how union and management can apply mutual
gains principles. Most of the authors of books on the market
reach a wider audience by presenting negotiations on the larger
scale. Unfortunately for collective bargaining negotiators, it is
difficult to translate what they are saying into union-management relationship terms.

This book focuses on moving beyond the walls of conflict.
It presents the need for union-management peace and the specifics of how to apply it in the real negotiating setting. For parties

who are considering alternative dispute resolution processes, it can be the road map, a tool for collective bargaining and union-management problem solving.

The following specific characteristics of *Beyond the Walls of Conflict* distinguish it from other works:

- It clearly spells out the benefits for management and union and identifies the situations in which this process may and may not work.

- It lists key success factors essential to union-management peace from the perspective of a practitioner rather than an academic.

- It distinctly contrasts union-management war and peace, showing the way negotiations would proceed through collective bargaining in both cases.

- It explores the sensitive topic of "trust and mistrust." Most books avoid this topic, while this work addresses it straightforwardly and explores how parties can build and destroy trust.

- It clearly articulates the steps to use in mutual gains negotiating. This includes how to plan for collective bargaining, how to get started, how to negotiate specific issues, how to reach agreement, and how to live by the agreement after the contract is signed.

- It explores specific negotiation traps as well as strategies to help negotiators recognize and respond to them. Also discussed are issues of how to get senior leadership buy-in and how the process can be undermined after the contract is signed.

- It presents a more futuristic direction of what the world looks like beyond the walls of conflict. In 1940, J. B. Priestley emphasized the evolution from power and property to community and creation. This work explores in earnest the way to establish union-management peace as a way of life. The organizations that can thrive on creation and community, and as Deming says "drive fear out of the organization," will be able to rise to the challenges of this decade and into the next century.

HOW TO USE THIS BOOK

Beyond the Walls of Conflict is written for management and union representatives interested in exploring alternative dispute resolution methods in their ongoing relationships and in their collective bargaining. Negotiators can use the book as:

- A method of creating interest to motivate them to consider an alternative kind of relationship in labor relations.

- A study guide text to be distributed as part of joint training or training within the company or the union.

- A guide to negotiators as they proceed through problem solving and collective bargaining.

- An explanation to members of the union and company management of the methods used in negotiations and the expectations of each party as they proceed to live by the agreements.

Another audience will be the academic community. Academics will finally have a book they can use to teach their students how to do collective bargaining using mutual gains negotiations.

STRUCTURE OF THE BOOK

The following is a brief statement of the purpose of each of the book's chapters:

Chapter 1: The Eighteenth Camel: Encourages rethinking about how to handle conflict and how this can be applied to the union-management arena.

Chapter 2: Union-Management War and Peace: Explores the characteristics of war and peace in labor relations and how they differ in collective bargaining.

Chapter 3: The Paradox of Trust and Mistrust: Describes the three stages of trust in negotiations, how to move from mistrust to trust, and how trust will be relevant in the ability to reach a mutual gains agreement.

Chapter 4: Planning for Successful Negotiations: Presents the planning steps for mutual gains negotiations in which the trust is high or low.

Chapter 5: Getting Started with Face-to-Face Negotiations: Clarifies how parties begin mutual gains negotiations to create union-management peace.

Chapter 6: Knowing and Understanding the Problem: Describes the steps required to identify the common interests and generate a joint problem statement to which the parties can agree.

Chapter 7: Discovering Creative Solutions: Explains how to generate common interest ideas and a joint solution.

Chapter 8: How to Reach an Agreement: Explores methods of reaching a mutual gains collective agreement and evaluating its quality.

Chapter 9: Negotiation Traps: Helps the reader spot seven negotiation traps and describes the proper strategies to avoid them if they are identified early enough.

Chapter 10: Beyond the Walls of Conflict: Suggests a new direction for management and union built on the creation of a new kind of community that supports ongoing union-management dialogue and joint governance.

The anecdotal comments in this book reflect the stories gleaned from the many companies and unions with which I have worked as a consultant. These stories bring the richness of those experiences to the reader. So come along and we will begin the journey together.

ACKNOWLEDGMENTS

Many people contributed to the concepts and stories in this manuscript, but without question the essential insights come from courageous union and management negotiators with whom I have worked. Their willingness to experiment with this approach and its successes and difficulties form the foundation of this narrative.

Specific negotiators and thinkers have also been very instrumental in the evolution of my thought process and application of mutual gains negotiations. To name a few: James Marchant, Richard Long, George Smith, and Dr. Bryan Downie have been very helpful in the idea development process. Other conceptual thinkers such as Dr. David Bakan and The Honourable Alan B. Gold added rigor to the generation and refinement of ideas. The Ontario Public School Boards' Association is also acknowledged for granting permission to the author to use the theme of their 1995 Conference as the title of this book.

My human resources and industrial relations consulting firm of Geller, Shedletsky and Weiss has been a backbone of support throughout this process. My partners, Dr. Ralph Shedletsky, Dr. Sheldon Geller, and Marijane Terry, supported this project from its inception. Françoise Morissette was a spirited supporter of this project, and Sylvia Odenwald and Mary Jo Beebe were extremely helpful in the promotion and editing of this work.

Finally, the inspiration for this book is from my wife, Dr. Nora Gold, and my son, Joseph Weissgold. To Nora: your love and friendship, along with your personal integrity, creativity, and tireless work for peace, have been an ongoing source of support for me and this project. And to Joseph, the little peace-maker: This book is a wish that the purity of your heart, percep-tiveness of your mind, and spirit of your soul help bring a little more peace and love to us all.

Dr. David S. Weiss

CONTENTS

CHAPTER 7

Discovering Creative Solutions   153

CHAPTER 8

How to Reach an Agreement   189

CHAPTER 1

The Eighteenth Camel

Many years ago, a man died and left his camels to his three sons; one-half to the oldest, one-third to the second son, and one-ninth to the youngest. However, there was a problem—he had only 17 camels.

A dispute quickly arose among the brothers. The eldest son argued that the father's will was in error because one-half, one-third, and one-ninth do not add up to a whole. He felt that he should receive all the camels because this was the tradition in the community. The middle son said his wife had the potential to be very ill and pleaded for an extra camel so that he could sustain his family. Although the story was not true, it seemed like a good idea at the time to get that extra camel at all costs and deal with the family fallout later. The youngest son argued that what was allocated to him was actually one-sixth because a number reversal had occurred.

The adversarial negotiation escalated. The feud became so heated that the families did not speak to each other. The brothers no longer allowed their children to play together and terminated all joint ventures between themselves. One of the siblings even thought of killing some of the camels or one of his brothers.

The brothers desperately needed to resolve this conflict. They finally agreed to go to a wise old woman in the community and tell her of their problem. They gave her the right to arbitrate their dispute and to dictate a solution. She said, "I am old and unable to ride my camel anymore. Why don't you take my camel? Then you will have 18 camels and you can divide them among the three of you."

The brothers gave half (or 9) of the 18 camels to the eldest son, a third (or 6) of them to the second son and a ninth (or 2) of them to the youngest son. One camel remained. The brothers were able to agree that they should return it to the old woman.

YOU DON'T HAVE TO LOSE FOR ME TO WIN

The objective of mutual gains negotiation is to discover that 18th camel. The "pie" is not fixed—what I get you do not lose. The image of a pie illustrates the available resources to be divided among the negotiating parties. The pie is fixed in adversarial negotiations—there are only 17 camels to divide and the solution is elusive. The only choice is concession or compromise in which no one wins. In mutual gains negotiations, the pie is not fixed. If parties think together, they can "expand the pie"; that is, increase the available resources and enlarge them to discover and distribute the 18th camel. The challenge is to discover a new solution, one that expands the pie and enables all the participants in a dispute to win, as did the brothers in the story.

The 18th camel story may sound all too magical and perhaps too simple. Sometimes the solution *is* simple. To see the solution, however, the parties must be willing to collaborate in order to discover their real interests. Also, they must want to use a joint problem-solving approach rather than a "demands, confrontation, and concession" method that at best produces compromise.

RETHINKING HOW TO HANDLE CONFLICT

Organizations are entering a new frontier where the potential for conflict is greater. Business boundaries inside and outside organizations are changing. As they blur or disappear altogether, the potential for conflict increases. On this new frontier, expertise in deal making, problem solving, negotiating, collaborating, and resolving conflicts determines the difference between success and failure.

Inside many organizations today, a move to an empowered workforce is shifting decision making from a top-down process to a more democratic one. In this environment, more people are contributing to decisions about what to do and how to do it. Traditional hierarchies are making way for self-directed work teams, quality management, continuous improvement programs, and mutual gains solutions. As a consequence, some organizations are experiencing more conflict, not less. Empowered employees are demanding more meaningful work and more input into decision making. Teams and employees are competing with each other for limited company resources. Decentralized departments are battling over intraorganizational decisions.

In addition to a shift in internal decision making, organizations are facing increased competition and globalization. The potential for conflict escalates when a company's global alliances result in a change to a multicultural environment or when a union aligns with a company for mutual gain.

The disputes that arise when one party does not play by the rules or seems to be getting more from the deal than the other are a major source of dysfunction in organizations. Managing relationships and resolving disputes after new alliances are forged require just as much time and as many resources as negotiating the new venture in the first place.

Organizations that hope to be counted among the winners will have to take a hard look at how they respond to conflict. Negotiating and conflict resolution skills have quickly reached core-competency status in today's organizations. These competencies are in demand not only in the day-to-day operations and leadership of the organization but in the union-management relationship as well.

Adversarial Negotiating Tactics Use Conflict to Resolve Conflict

Traditional bargaining is often adversarial. The strongest idea wins—not the better one. Resolving conflict through collaboration and seeking common ground often loses to coercion. The method most often used has been to manage conflict with conflict. Parties state strong positions, draw battle lines, and then center their discussions on the proposal favored by one party or the other. Lip service is paid to finding mutually satisfying solutions. Frequently, more energy is spent identifying the opponent's weaknesses than thinking about maximizing joint gains. In this environment, it is natural to be adversarial and unnatural to trust others. Only imposed social order is effective at suppressing this confrontational drive.

Whether one company is suing another company or a union is negotiating with management, adversarial tactics are usually very time-consuming and costly. They produce winners and losers or, at best, inadequate compromise in which all parties believe they have lost.

More Collaborative Approaches Achieve Wise Solutions at Less Expense

In recent years, a poor economy has been the impetus for more collaborative methods of negotiating. Organizations simply cannot *afford* to lose. A conflict resolution model that results in winners and losers is not good enough in today's economy. Even the winners are not guaranteed a long-term gain if hidden agendas are disguised during negotiation—only to erupt and disrupt later.

More legal disputes are also being settled out of court by means of third-party processes. Traditional negotiation rituals involving numerous lawyers and lasting many months or even years are being replaced by new approaches that use a mediator or facilitator to achieve agreement faster and with less expense.

Faced with a sobering socioeconomic environment, restructuring, downsizing, more competition, government social contracts, and threats to job security, unions and management have begun to work together to address common concerns. It may be just a marriage of convenience, but in some situations both sides have shifted away from their traditional adversarial roles to ensure organizational competitiveness and labor peace.

It's Time to Rethink Win-Lose Strategies That Threaten Trust in Relationships

Conventional win-lose strategies may achieve agreement but at the expense of trust and an ongoing relationship. Emphasis should be on determining *what* is right, not *who* is right—on discussing problems, not arguing positions.

Problems and threats can be turned into opportunities through negotiating to achieve mutual gains. The basic characteristics of mutual gains negotiations are eminently reasonable. In mutual gains negotiations, both parties do the following:

- Take ownership and responsibility for the outcome of the negotiation.
- Work to keep the relationship intact.
- Work on problems rather than make demands.
- Use processes to deliberately stimulate creative solutions.
- Work together to create solutions in which all parties benefit.

Conflict puts opposing parties at a disadvantage because their thinking becomes rigid and they are seldom able to see

situations from other than their own perspective. Using traditional adversarial bargaining, with no requirements for joint work,
the most they can hope to achieve is compromise.

UNION-MANAGEMENT PEACE AT WORK

Increased competition is forcing companies and unions to think
differently about how they handle disputes. To respond to the
current challenges, they are exploring ways to collaborate. Union-
management peace has become one of the core strategies to save
companies and ensure job security for employees.

In the book *The Mutual Gains Enterprise,* Kochan and
Osterman argue for a business transformation. They suggest that
the role of unions, government, and human resource professionals be expanded to transform the enterprise's competitiveness.
They argue that in enlightened organizations, the company and
union can achieve mutual gains. The union can contribute to an
increase in productivity and quality, be a "powerful force for
sustaining commitment to workplace innovations," and "institu-
tionalize these innovations to the point they produce significant
benefits to the enterprise."[1]

Nevertheless, Kochan and Osterman think the work councils used in Germany are the greatest area of opportunity for
mutual gains. Their book explores how the mutual gains opportunity can work through the collective bargaining process. It
functions as a conceptual and practical guide to unions and
companies in this exciting experiment of workplace reform.

The Role of Human Resource Professionals in Workplace Reform

Originally, human resource departments were created to reduce
the risk of having incompetent people in organizations. That role
was sufficient when the companies were growing. In times of
dramatic transformation, however, the role of human resource
professionals has expanded to include the creation of an adaptive

culture. This means that the human resource department must act as the catalyst for change. It sets the context and readiness for the changes senior management will introduce in order to compete in the decade ahead.

One of the prime areas of transformation is in the relationship between companies and unions. Many companies speak of their employees as their most valuable asset and their unions as a major liability. Works such as that of Kochan and Osterman demonstrate what is already known to some professionals: Having a union-management partnership to reach mutual gains solutions and union-management peace can be a strategic advantage for the company, the union, and the employees.

WHY UNION-MANAGEMENT PEACE AT THIS TIME?

No one transforms an organization and moves toward a more peaceful coexistence for strictly benevolent reasons. Even a saint seeks personal reward, if not in this life, then in the world to come. Companies and unions see gains that can be made by moving from an adversarial relationship to one built on union-management peace.

What's in It for the Companies?

There are many benefits for a company. (Note: The comments about companies in this book can also be applied to nonprofit organizations and to government agencies and departments.) Up until five years ago, companies rarely entered a collective bargaining session with proposals of their own. Their primary objective was to survive the negotiations with a minimum amount of loss. They never considered the possibility of gain. To achieve their vision of the status quo, they had to negotiate for a period of time—sometimes as long as three months.

Many companies negotiated with the hope that they would not give away more than the unions already had. They operated under the principle of status quo negotiating, which is, "The longer you negotiate, the more you give away." It then became management's objective to find delay tactics, little tricks that would allow them to postpone negotiations. If the negotiations proceeded with delay tactics, the legal requirement for negotiation would be met. The result was that they would be negotiating in name only, when in reality they had not negotiated at all.

To delay, companies often assigned negotiators who were new and, therefore, would have a slow learning curve. They did not assign people to the negotiation table who were able to make decisions because then the pace of the negotiations could be escalated. The decision makers were always outside the room so that the process would drag on. Only in the last weeks before the negotiation deadline did management get serious. They knew they had to make a deal to avoid a work stoppage and to develop a new financial package.

The situation is different now. Companies bring proposals to the negotiation table that are really demands in disguise. Organizations need change to compete. They require more flexibility in the way work is assigned, multiskilling, pay-for-performance, and the creation of the contract, which will allow for human resource professionals to build adaptive cultures. Without a change in the union-management relationship, an adaptive culture, which is vital for competitiveness, will be inaccessible. Companies need union-management peace in order to survive.

What's in It for the Unions?

While companies were trying to escape negotiations, unions were getting extremely frustrated by their avoidance tactics. They resorted to subversive acts of their own. They did not learn them from companies alone. Long ago, a book by Saul Alinsky, *Reveille for Radicals*,[2] gave information about extreme tactics to use. The reciprocity of mistrust escalated. Negotiations were an embarrassment for both company and union representatives and caused excessive stress, heartache, and often dissatisfying results for all parties.

As business has become more competitive, the entire corporate enterprise is being threatened. The competition is *between* companies as well as *within* companies. Political free-trade zones are closing plants as manufacturing moves southward. Within companies, plants are competing for the capacity to produce and service products, resulting in plant closings and massive layoffs. This competitiveness threatens jobs and security, which is the core reason for the existence of unions.

Some unions have recognized a strategic advantage of collaborative negotiations—that they minimize plant closings. Through these negotiations, unions gain security for their membership and for themselves as political leaders of the collective employee body. Working toward union-management peace though mutual gains negotiations becomes the new route to plant and job security.

Employees are also demanding that their job responsibilities be expanded and their skills upgraded so they can compete with new and younger workers who are more technologically proficient. They recognize that there are no more jobs for life and that they cannot leave their career management to the companies or the unions. They need to take ownership of their own career cycles and ensure their own employability as they move into the future.

Another specific advantage unions gain in this time of change is a greater voice in decision making. Union representatives, or people nominated by the unions, are now on boards of directors of many companies—particularly in the airline industry. What used to be anathema to the unions has now become the vogue; they now want to be in the decision-making process and contribute directly to the future direction of companies. Union-management peace is now vital to the survival and security of employees and unions.

KEY SUCCESS FACTORS IN UNION-MANAGEMENT PEACE

Specific success factors contribute to an effective union-management peace process. Without them, the likelihood of success is greatly diminished.

Follow the Mutual Gains Process

Focusing on the mutual gains process is necessary for success. An interesting analogy that illustrates this principle is that of a driver of a car skidding into a ditch. Her survival depends on her focus. If she looks toward the ditch, she is more likely to steer into it than if she looks toward the road.

Negotiating parties need to focus on specific mutual gains processes in order to succeed. Only after they are very comfortable with the process can they stray effectively from the defined way of doing it.

Sometimes, at the outset of negotiations, parties use a facilitator to help them stay with the process. A neutral third party can help achieve mutual gains and innovative solutions without acting as a go-between or a judge. Using effective facilitation, the facilitator orchestrates the union-management negotiation by using processes to:

- Uncover each party's real objectives.
- Assist each side to see the other's perspective.
- Explore options beyond the barriers established by the problem.

Whenever possible, they transfer these skills and techniques to all parties to enhance their ability to prevent future conflict and to manage the process without help.

Conduct Joint Union-Management Training

Joint training, when done well, is an essential ingredient in building relationships and trust between negotiating parties. The negotiations actually begin during the training when parties explore how they will negotiate by studying negotiation cases and real examples. The pattern set in the joint training can be used as a model for the actual negotiations. Parties can refer back to the model to keep on course.

Have the Right People Negotiating

The right people need to be at the table doing the negotiations. One can easily predict how the process will proceed by looking at the negotiators at the table. In an adversarial negotiation, decision makers or people who have to live with the contract after it is signed are rarely the ones who are bargaining at the negotiating table. It is more common to see professional nego-tiators or "middlemen" who do not make decisions but rather operate as messengers for decision makers outside the room. In mutual gains negotiations, a key to success is to have negotiators who can make decisions at the negotiating table and who will have to live with the results of the contract.

In most cases, mutual gains negotiators include people who:

- Can make decisions at the table or at least present strong recommendations that are more likely to be accepted.
- Are line supervisors and union representatives.
- All parties can respect.

Build the Mutual Gains Approach into the Contract to Make It a "Right"

Negotiators come and go. One fear of unions and companies is that when the economic situation changes they may lose the peace they achieve at this unique time of transition. One effective strategy has been to write the intent of union-management peace into the contract. The more profile it receives, the better. Some contracts include values statements up front as well as the agreed-upon common interests around which future disputes can be resolved.

With the mutual gains approach to union-management peace written into the contract, the desire for a new relationship will outlive its authors. It becomes a new bill of rights to which the company, the union, and the employees can refer as they venture into uncharted territory.

Build the Mutual Gains Approach into the Ongoing Management-Employee Relationship

The collective bargaining process can potentially be an alternate route to culture change in the company. To achieve union-management peace, the change cannot stop with the collective bargaining process. The discontinuity between contract negotiations and the day-to-day management-employee relationship will become a significant barrier if the gap is not reduced quickly. The changes that occur in collective bargaining must be reflected in the daily interactions between all managers and employees.

Mutual gains problem solving has to become the way of working on a day-to-day basis. Through mutual gains problem solving, unions and employees become active partners with management in creating quality processes and continuous improvements. They share a common understanding of the work community they are trying to build. All parties benefit with additional security, profitability, and customer satisfaction.

GIVE UNION-MANAGEMENT PEACE A CHANCE

Any model designed for dispute resolution has advantages and disadvantages. No one approach is the answer to every situation. Many successful contracts have been negotiated using traditional bargaining. But, in this new global and competitive environment in which the potential for conflict has increased, mutual gains negotiating offers optimum results. These results go far beyond an adversarial approach and can achieve new benefits through union-management peace.

To emphasize the need for global political change, John Lennon once sang, "All we are saying, is give peace a chance." In the workplace, it's now up to union and management. Discover the 18th camel and give peace a chance. It's worth it!

SUMMARY

- The objective of mutual gains negotiation is to discover the 18th camel.

- Organizations that hope to be counted among the winners will have to take a hard look at how they respond to conflict.

- Traditional bargaining is often adversarial.

- In recent years, a poor economy has been the impetus for more collaborative methods of negotiating.

- Conventional win-lose strategies may achieve agreement but at the expense of trust and an ongoing relationship.

- Increased competition is forcing companies and unions to think differently about how they handle disputes. They are exploring ways to collaborate in order to respond to the current challenges.

- Without a change in the union-management relationship, the adaptive culture, which is vital for competitiveness, will be inaccessible.

- Some unions have recognized a strategic advantage of collaborative negotiations—that they minimize work stoppage.

- Companies and unions need union-management peace in order to survive.

- Specific success factors contribute to an effective union-management peace process.
  - Follow the mutual gains process.
  - Conduct joint union-management training.
  - Have the right people negotiating.
  - Build the mutual gains approach into the contract to make it a "right."

- Build the mutual gains approach into the ongoing management-employee relationship.
- Mutual gains negotiating offers results that go far beyond an adversarial approach and can achieve new benefits through union-management peace.

CHAPTER 2

Union-Management War and Peace

The field of union-management relations is filled with war stories. Some of them are bizarre, some are funny, and others are tragic. I have chosen to provide these narratives without identifying the companies or unions. To paraphrase Pete Seeger, who allegedly said to the House Un-American Committee, "I won't name names but I'll sing you a song." I won't name names either, but I'll tell you the stories.

One of the many tales told among union-management negotiators is about an adversarial negotiation in which the parties tried to close an agreement after the deadline had passed. A company and union negotiator were doing the last-minute negotiations. The remainder of the negotiators stayed in the area because they had to sign the memorandum of agreement.

When the two parties finally settled at 3:00 A.M., the other negotiators' signatures were required. It was evident that one of the negotiators was drunk. The others assisted him to the table, propped him up, put a pen between his fingers, and helped him scribble his name on the agreement. He then collapsed on the table, where he slept for the rest of the night.

That is just one of many stories union-management negotiators tell and retell. Adversarial negotiations create great theater—but more is at stake than theatrics. The union-management

encounter, whether it is warlike or peaceful, makes a great difference for employees, union, management, negotiators, and the
company. Peace may not be as mediaworthy as war, but its
benefits are vast for all parties.

An essential capability needed to achieve union-management peace is skill in mutual gains negotiating and problem
solving. Mutual gains negotiating is not easy, nor is it a giveaway
program; it is a very tough method of dispute resolution. It
requires concentration, a focus, and a problem-solving orienta-
tion. While hard work is necessary, mutual gains negotiating has
the potential to yield very beneficial results to all parties and
contribute to union-management peace.

INTERESTS, RIGHTS, AND POWER

Mutual gains negotiations differ from traditional adversarial
negotiations in important ways:

- The focus is on resolving real problems—rather than
  trading demands.
- Success is based on the merits of the case—not on
  power.
- Parties present their problems and discuss them to try
  to discover a joint creative solution that meets the
  common interests—rather than making self-serving
  demands.

Adversarial and mutual gains negotiations are similar in
that both involve the same approaches to negotiating—interests,
rights, and power. They differ dramatically, though, in how and
when interests, rights, and power are used.

As you can see in Figure 2–1, the same approaches are used.
The difference is the order in which the negotiators use the
approaches. Most negotiators are fully able to use power, rights,
and interests, but they need to explore using these approaches
in the reverse order.

FIGURE 2–1

Interests, Rights, and Power

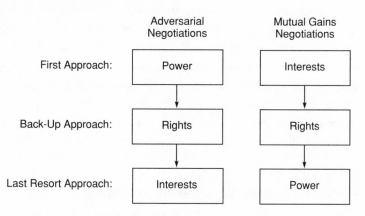

The "18th camel" story describes a typical adversarial negotiation. It begins with a power approach, which is typical of adversarial negotiations. Only after the power approach fails do parties begin to explore their rights and argue for the external verification that supports their positions. As a last resort, parties explore interests—often over a drink in a one-on-one communication.

In mutual gains negotiations, the process is the reverse. Parties begin with the discovery of underlying common interests. If that is unsuccessful, they can resort to the rights approach. Only if all else fails do they use power to try to resolve the dispute. Negotiators do not give up power in mutual gains negotiation; they use it as a last resort.

What Is an Interest Approach?

In mutual gains negotiating, the interest approach is the first method for communicating with your counterparts. In adversarial negotiations, you use the interest approach only as a last resort. Much of this book is devoted to understanding how to use this approach as a way to achieve union-management peace.

The interest approach ensures that negotiators deal with problems and not demands. They share information, identify common interests, explain why they want a particular solution, and generate overall agreements that provide for mutual gains—even if those gains are not equivalent for each issue. The interest approach focuses on answering the question, "What is important to you in negotiations?" The needs that are uncovered as a result of answering this question must be met.

To achieve mutual gains using the interest approach, negotiators are guided by three core principles:[3]

- Develop wise solutions.
- Identify the simplest possible solutions.
- Enhance the quality of the relationship between the parties.

"Wise solutions" are those that effectively answer the problem the parties address. When using the interest approach, negotiators *resolve problems;* they do not *negotiate demands.* The wise mutual gains solution is the right one in the situation. It is not based on personalities or who wins or loses.

The principle is to negotiate *what* is right, not *who* is right. It is important to search for the right answer—the wise answer rather than whose turn it is to win. In grievance situations, for example, parties may aggressively pursue a decision in their favor to enhance their political track record. If they lost the last 10 grievances, they may believe it is their turn to win one regardless of the merits of the existing case. In mutual gains negotiating, the worthiness of the case, not the scorecard, determines resolution.

"Simple solutions" are wise solutions that are understood when communicated and have an excellent possibility of being implemented in the way they were agreed to. Simple solutions enhance the probability that the parties will live by their decisions after they sign the contract. Because the parties understand the solution, they can plan how they will work together effectively throughout the duration of the agreement.

Complex agreements break the unwritten rule of negotiating—you never reach an agreement your first-line supervisors and stewards cannot implement. Often the language of an agreed-to solution is too complex for these individuals to determine their intent. The result is numerous grievances. Simple solutions result in fewer grievances, making union-management peace more possible.

The "quality of the relationships is enhanced" as a result of the trust that is built by negotiators who clarify expectations and deliver what is expected. As a result, parties understand each other better and appreciate what each brings to the situation. By establishing a strong relationship, they are more likely to continue negotiations afterwards and to resolve disputes. A strong relationship also enhances the likelihood that the next time parties negotiate, they will be able to use mutual gains principles and sustain union-management peace.

All three guiding principles are necessary and essential. If a solution is simple and enhances the relationship but is not wise, its weaknesses will be evident when it is implemented. If the solution is wise and enhances the relationship but is not simple, only the negotiators will understand its intent. As a result, confusion will reign among others who will work with it on a daily basis. Finally, if the solution is wise and simple but does not enhance the relationship, the parties will be unable to leverage this success for ongoing and continuous negotiations.

What Is the Rights Approach?

The preferred method in mutual gains negotiations is to resolve conflicts using an interest approach without having to resort to a rights approach. Nevertheless, there are times when rights are necessary and even desirable as an effective buffer from the immediate application of power. In addition, most negotiations begin with references to rights, the collective agreement, the will, precedents, and so on, which represent what each party believes the other has a duty to provide. Once the parties are working within the problem, however, the rights approach becomes a second line of defense.

A rights approach is a method of resolving conflict based on involving either a third party or an external information source. The simplest example is arbitration in which parties bring a grievance to an arbitrator. At that point the parties are beyond interests. They are basing their case on rights arguments. They are looking for what the other party has a duty to provide as a result of legal precedent, trends, patterns in the community—whatever strategy possible to convince the arbitrator they have the better case and, therefore, should win in the dispute resolution process. When a solution is based on rights, there are winners and losers. In most cases, a fixed pie is distributed to the disputing parties. The rights approach focuses on answering the question, "What is the duty the other party must meet or the precedent on which I will base my case?"

Some examples of rights arguments include:

- The collective agreement.
- Prevailing custom and tradition.
- Legal precedent.
- Third-party mediation or judgment of the situation.
- Standards and criteria.
- A challenge to another party's claims to rights.
- Past experience.
- Pattern bargaining in which what another group received through a similar negotiation is the baseline for this negotiation process.
- A strike or a lockout. As the former Superior Court Chief Justice of Quebec, the Honourable Alan B. Gold, says: "The right to strike (save the exceptions where it does not and should not exist) is an integral part of the system and if you remove or impair it, you necessarily alter the system itself."[4] Although mutual gains negotiation alters the system, it does not eliminate the

collective agreement, the right to strike or, for that matter, the right to lock out.

When to apply the rights approach raises controversy among experts in the area of mutual gains negotiations. For example, in the highly-acclaimed book *Getting to Yes* by Fisher and Ury, the authors suggest that standards or rights be used as one method of assessing the quality of an interest-based solution.[5] The weakness of that criterion, though, is that it introduces the quality of a rights solution. The preferred strategy is to identify the benefits and risks of an interest-based solution and try to resolve the conflict based on interests.

The rights approach in adversarial negotiations is abused when both parties search out rights or standards that support their position only and that vary dramatically from those of the other party. The classic example is psychiatric testimony in the courtroom. The prosecutor finds a psychiatrist to claim that a defendant is mentally competent, while the defense attorney finds another equally qualified psychiatrist to maintain that the defendant is psychiatrically disabled. Both are making a rights argument based on legal precedent and expert opinion. Both lawyers find the expert opinion that supports their case only and are not looking for a fair standard to use as a measure of whether the person is mentally competent. That kind of rights manipulation is one reason why some people may mistrust lawyers.

As one Ontario court judge wrote in the beginning of a judgment: "The conclusion that I must reach is that, depending on the definition I adopt, arbitration and the right to sue may involve different things but they may not."[6] Rights can be turned to a party's advantage very easily. Clearly, it's better to try to resolve the dispute within the realm of the interest approach.

Some argue that the term "mutual gains negotiations" implies that no rights should be specified through the collective agreement contract (not surprisingly, the argument comes from management). Quite the contrary, there will always be a contract and a dispute resolution process in mutual gains negotiations. The content of the contract may be driven by values and intent rather than rules, but it will still be a collective labor agreement contract.

The contract of the future exists now in some organizations. The GM Saturn and United Auto Workers contract is a case in point. The contract is only 28 pages long and focuses heavily on values and intent. There are similar contracts available in the public domain such as those between Stelco Inc. and the United Steelworkers; AT&T and the CWA/IBEW; Bell Canada and the Communication, Energy and Paperworkers Union of Canada; and Domtar Packaging and the Independent Paperworkers of Canada, to name a few.

These collective labor agreements will continue to have grievance procedures for legitimate concerns that arise periodically. But the companies and unions may find the number of grievances reduced. They may also discover that they have greater ability to negotiate continuously on issues rather than escalating to a level that will hurt the company and the employees. Many of these contracts also have a due process used to interpret the contract.

The collective labor agreement provides another additional invaluable advantage. It functions like the courts do in most societies. Parties often resolve disputes without having to go to court. When they cannot reach a solution, however, the courts are safe havens for resolving disputes so that they do not escalate to an uncivilized level. Without the right to litigate, the only resolution strategy is to impose power. Just as the courts provide a peaceful way to buffer the immediate application of power, the collective labor agreement is a right that restrains litigants from regressing to power approaches. The contract is useful and essential to support the mutual gains negotiations agreement between the company and its unions.

What Is the Power Approach?

Perhaps one of the most comforting aspects of the mutual gains approach is that parties do not relinquish power if they proceed through interests and rights. Countries that choose to make peace treaties do not dismantle their military. As Yehoshaphat Harkabi formerly of the Israeli Mossad Intelligence says, "You never make peace treaties between friends."[7] The objective is not to have the two parties become best of friends or even one team; it is simply to bring negotiated peace.

Power is much more effective before it's used than after. Even the guru of adversarial negotiations, Saul Alinsky, says in his tactics chapter of *Rules for Radicals* that "the threat is more terrifying than the thing itself."[8] Power, once used, is lost. It is not a replenishable resource. That argument alone is compelling parties to apply power only as a last resort and to find an 18th camel based upon common interests.

The use of power, then, is rare in the mutual gains environment. It is much more common in adversarial negotiating. The power approach has some downsides. If negotiators engage in adversarial negotiations, they use power to ensure they win and the other party loses, regardless of the longer-term implications. The power approach focuses on answering the question, "What do you want; what is your demand?" The objective of those who use this approach is to achieve those ends regardless of the means.

The strategies used in the power approach are numerous and, on occasion, even ritualized. Some classic ones are:

- **Using emotion, anger, and guilt as a manipulative strategy.** When parties use the power approach, it is common for them to shout at each other and use dramatics such as walking out of the room and swearing.

- **Using deception to defend a demand.** Parties may not even know the reason for their demands or may choose not to explain the true reasons for their demands.

- **Playing personality or "head" games as a way to manipulate the other party to weaken its position.** Reading newspapers during negotiations or yelling and screaming are examples of games played to manipulate to personal advantage.

- **Employing symbolic gestures that embarrass or send messages.** An example of this technique occurred in a recent union-management negotiation. During the management's financial presentation, union members munched on buttered popcorn. The smell in the room was unbearable. When the union representatives were asked why they were eating popcorn, they replied, "Because we came to see the show!"

- **Exerting physical or psychological force.** Intimidation is part of the power approach. In one situation, the chief negotiator for the union leaned forward in a threatening way. The chief spokesperson for the company leaped backwards, assuming that the union representative was about to make a physical attack. The union spokesperson laughed and said, "I was only putting on my boots."

- **Withholding information to increase power.** In traditional bargaining, knowledge is power. The more parties withhold information, the more powerful they are. In the absence of real information, however, the other party will fabricate information, which only makes the situation worse.

- **Using an ultimatum.** Threats are common in the power approach. Good power negotiators never use threats unless they mean what they say. If they yield to pressure, future threats and ultimatums will be meaningless. Even in the power approach, ultimatums based on bluffs are inadvisable.

- **Using delay tactics to avoid negotiating.** This strategy described earlier is used for status quo negotiations. The delay looks like negotiations, but nothing is really happening.

- **Applying divide-and-conquer techniques.** The purpose of this strategy is to divide the members of the opposing party and provoke them to fight among themselves. Parties often accomplish this by swaying a major influencer of their opposition to their side. The influencer then manipulates his or her counterparts to acquiesce to the other side's demands.

If the objective of the parties in a power dispute is simply to get what they want at any cost, they are not concerned about the means or the ethics. Saul Alinsky says that "in war the ends justify almost any means."[9] All the above strategies are used in adversarial negotiations, even if they may not be ethical.

The elegant negotiator uses the power approach with an astute sense of timing, knowing exactly when to move to rights and interests. Even in the power approach, the deal is struck on interests no matter how little time is allocated to the interest discussions.

In mutual gains negotiations, parties rarely use power and only when there is no other choice. During the planning process, parties independently explore how much power they have. When the parties believe they have equal power, mutual gains negotiating is the logical approach to problem resolution. But even when one party has more power than the other, they still should exercise their power only if negotiations fail after they have used the interest and rights approaches.

When to Move from the Interest Approach to Rights and Power

One of the biggest challenges mutual gains negotiators face is to determine when the interest approach is not working and, therefore, when to use the rights and power approaches. In addition, if negotiators have to use rights and power, they must make sure these approaches do not sabotage mutual gains negotiations for the next problem they encounter.

The minimum standard for an interest-based solution to a problem is that it has to be at least equal to or better than what the parties believe they would have negotiated with a rights or power approach. Excellent mutual gains negotiators apply this test regularly. They know the constituencies they represent will apply that test as well. Union membership and management will ask, "Could we have done better if we had negotiated the old way?" If the answer is yes, then the mutual gains negotiators are in trouble. If the interest approach solutions are as good as what would have emerged from the rights or power approaches, then the solutions are acceptable, primarily because they have also enhanced the relationship.

At times, the mutual gains negotiator does not apply the above test. That omission has hurt revenue and employee satisfaction for both the company and the union. For example, a service company announced it would downsize. Rather than submit to a layoff of 10 percent of the workforce, the union became involved and negotiated an agreement that reduced the workweek to four and a half days. When the agreement was announced, line management, employees, and customers were disturbed. Line management was shocked at the change negotiated without consultation, employees were upset with the reduction of work and pay (especially those not targeted for the downsizing), and customers were furious that service was reduced. What seemed like a mutual gains solution was really a mutual loss for everyone. It narrowly passed a union ratification vote.

The situation got worse. Because of customer demand, the company had to pay time and a half for employees to work the extra half day. Operating costs went up, employee morale went down, and customers were still unhappy dealing with disgruntled employees.

Sigmund Freud once said that when it comes to self-deception, people are geniuses. The negotiators should have tested their solution to see if it was equal to or better than the solutions that might have emerged from a rights or power approach. Doing this would have enabled them to see the weakness in their agreement. They had a simple solution that enhanced their relationship, but their answer was not wise and ultimately cost all parties dearly.

If mutual gains negotiators resort to rights or power, they should analyze the strength of their relationship with the other party and determine whether they will be able to use the interest approach for the next problem. Negotiators should be explicit about why a rights or power approach is being applied, communicate that these approaches are a last resort, and express the hope that the relationship can survive the crisis. The trust the parties build doing this will pay dividends if and when the next problem occurs.

COMPARING ADVERSARIAL AND MUTUAL GAINS NEGOTIATIONS

Adversarial and mutual gains negotiations differ in these areas:

- Training method.
- A common language of negotiation.
- Preparation by the parties for the negotiations.
- How negotiations begin.
- Negotiating style.
- Nature of the ongoing dialogue.
- Documentation and language.
- Method of reaching agreement.

Figure 2–2 summarizes the major contrasts between adversarial and mutual gains negotiations.

Training Method

In *adversarial negotiations,* the two parties to the dispute are trained separately. As a result, each party has a different language, agenda, and strategy of negotiations. In *mutual gains negotiations,* the two parties participate in joint training, which is often nonbinding. This means that the parties are not necessarily committing to proceed in this manner after the training process. Instead, they are learning together how they might bargain in a way that will benefit both of them.

FIGURE 2-2

Adversarial versus Mutual Gains Negotiations

	Adversarial Negotiations	Mutual Gains Negotiations
Training	• Separate training for company and union bargaining team	• Joint company/union
Focus	• Exchange formal demands/proposals	• Joint identification of issues/problems • Common objectives
Process for Negotiations	• Formal • Sit on opposite side of the bargaining table • Bound by what is said	• Informal • No bargaining table • Team approach • Nonbinding discussion • Mutual gains process used for analysis/resolution
Ongoing Dialogue	• Confrontational/party line	• Joint problem solving • Openness and candor • Out of character at times
Documentation	• Ongoing verbatim notes	• Flip charts used as memory joggers
Reaching Agreement	• Language signed during negotiations when agreement is reached for each point • Memorandum signed on completion	• No language signed until agreement is reached on everything • Memorandum signed on completion

The benefits of common training to the participants are numerous and include:

- A common language of negotiation.
- Relationships built during training that enhance the trust level the parties will have when they actually begin bargaining.

- Groundwork laid for ongoing mutual gains bargaining after training. Because discussion of real issues takes place during training, nonbinding negotiations occur in a nonthreatening environment.

A Common Language of Negotiation

In *adversarial negotiations,* the parties develop their own code of communication. While they send signals to each other from time to time, miscommunications are rampant. Parties place more emphasis on how something was said and the language used than on content.

In *mutual gains negotiations,* the joint training process and ongoing dialogue help the negotiating parties develop a language they both can understand. Miscommunications are reduced because together they learn the concepts of negotiating with each other as well as a common terminology.

Some of the more important language used includes "wise solutions that are simple and enhance the relationship" as well as the terms "interests, rights, and power approaches" to help them identify what is being said.

Some negotiating parties develop a common language to control the process of the meeting. In one dispute resolution situation, for example, the parties created code words to help them work together. Some of the terms they used and their definitions were:

- **"Ah-Ha" List.** This is a list of great ideas to be addressed later. Other people sometimes call these ideas the "parking lot."
- **"Sore Thumb" List.** This list has the items that are very painful and need to be dealt with at some time. Dealing with them now would take the parties off the topic and reduce their ability to focus on the problem at hand. By documenting them on the flip chart, the negotiators guarantee they will deal with them eventually.

- **A Rat Hole.** Going down a rat hole occurs when the parties discuss a contentious topic that is not related to the negotiations. This causes unnecessary tension and distraction.

- **Tape Loop.** In a tape loop, two people who are arguing repeat their statements several times. Often, they become louder and louder in an effort to assert their positions. They get nowhere and everyone becomes frustrated. Someone identifies the argument as a tape loop. The two parties stop and a third person offers comments.

- **Getting into the Bark.** This code word is used when the negotiators get into too much detail before the concept is fully understood (i.e., they get into the bark before seeing the forest and the trees).

- **Violent Agreement.** Sometimes two people sound as if they are arguing, but in reality they are agreeing. When someone points out that the two have reached a violent agreement, they tend to stop arguing.

Another group of negotiators who were enthusiastic hockey fans added these code words:

- **Time-out.** Anyone can call a time-out at any time for any reason.

- **Offsides.** Someone is pushing the other party too fast.

- **Two Minutes for Roughing.** Someone is so aggressive that he or she is called for a penalty, has to leave the table, and sit quietly for two minutes.

Preparation by the Parties for the Negotiation

In *adversarial negotiations*, parties often survey the people they represent to determine the demands they want to make. The parties then compile these demands for presentation to their adversaries. Their understanding of the constituents' demands and why they are important may be limited. In preparation for the negotiations, the parties may actually fabricate reasons why their demands are reasonable and present these contrived reasons during the negotiations process. The subtle deceptions need to be supported throughout the negotiations and can actually lead the negotiations into some very difficult territory. If the parties present verifiable deceptions, then trust is destroyed and neither party will believe the other.

In *mutual gains negotiating,* the parties survey their constituencies to discover the problems needing resolution. The parties collect their constituencies' problems, as well as what they think might be their potential solutions, and formulate the list of problems they believe will be relevant in the negotiations process. When the negotiations begin, both parties present the problems they would like to resolve. They generate a common list that forms the agenda of what they want to achieve in this round of negotiations.

How Negotiations Begin

In *adversarial negotiations,* parties prepare extensively prior to negotiations to put together formal demands. For example, in a union-management dispute it is not uncommon for a union to submit 100 to 300 demands, often with "a," "b," and "c" categories below each demand. It is a very careful and thorough analysis of every article within the collective agreement, with the union's recommendations for changes. Invariably, the company understands many of the demands but doesn't find them acceptable. The company also presents its demands, referred to as "proposals," which are often far fewer in number than the union's.

In an adversarial negotiation, the opening presentation can be quite dramatic and very political, with each side table stomping, attacking the other party verbally, and making very strong demands. Each side may accuse the other of lying, deceiving, and bargaining in bad faith. The climate is extremely adversarial and highly politicized.

Invariably, in adversarial negotiations there is very little discussion about the demands. Sometimes a party may ask the other party for clarification. However, the reply often provides only a limited explanation that makes it impossible for the opposing party to develop a fair response. On other occasions, a party may embellish an explanation because the real reason will be unacceptable to his or her counterpart.

Little discussion occurs at the negotiating table. The parties analyze the demands and prepare responses in their own back rooms. The real work is done outside the negotiating room. Once the parties return, they present their answers to the demands, often rejecting most of them. A climate of mistrust is established and becomes very difficult to break as the parties proceed with the bargaining process.

In one round of adversarial negotiating, the company spokesperson placed yellow "stickies"—each marked with the letters "NFW"—on many of the union's demands. The union representatives saw the company spokesperson's briefcase during a break and interpreted the letters to mean "No F—ing Way." They accused the company spokesperson of rejecting the union's demands before hearing the basis for them. The company spokesperson laughed and said that the union had misunderstood the meaning of the letters—that "NFW" meant "Needs Further Work."[10] You can be the judge of whom to believe.

In *mutual gains negotiations,* the process is very different. The parties are trained together and some trust and common understanding have already developed through that process. The fact that the parties are willing to proceed with mutual gains negotiations demonstrates some level of trust.

In mutual gains negotiations, both parties make opening statements that include why they want to proceed with mutual gains negotiating and their hope for the success of the process. The parties then present what they think the ground rules for negotiations should be. These ground rules are not meant to be negotiated items but rather principles of how they would like to proceed.

The following are typical negotiating ground rules:

- Participation by everyone.
- Honesty and no deceptions.
- Joint communications (eliminate negotiating through the media).
- Anyone can facilitate the discussions.
- Flip charts to be used as memory joggers.
- No hidden agendas.

Both parties present their ground rules, merge those rules, and then record them on flip charts. The charts are hung on the wall for the duration of the negotiations.

The parties then identify the agenda of problems they will tackle in the negotiations. This exercise takes quite a few days, depending on the complexity of the negotiations. The parties separate the problems into groups and then address each group in a different phase of the negotiations.

Usually, the clustered problems are sequenced, starting with those that reflect several common interests and progressing to those that have very few. The parties work first on those problems they believe reflect common interests. By doing this, they establish a preliminary level of trust before they have to handle the problems that appear to have fewer common interests.

The Negotiating Style

In *adversarial negotiations,* the parties sit on opposite sides of a rectangular table. As many as 20 people are on each side of the table with the chief spokespeople sitting at the center peering at one another. Usually, only the spokespeople do the talking. Often, each side appoints someone to record every word that is said. Each side also assigns negotiators the task of observing their counterparts' nonverbal clues in order to determine what to take seriously. You can imagine the restraint with which people speak—or even move. They try to avoid being spontaneous because they will be held accountable for every word they say or any movement they make.

If people speak out of turn during these negotiations or disagree with their chief spokesperson, they are usually corrected privately by the spokesperson for being inappropriate and breaking the trust within the negotiating group. The style is very tense, very political, and very aggressive. The focus is on personalities, which plays a critical role in how the agreement will be struck.

In *mutual gains negotiations,* the seating arrangements are often very informal. Instead of using a bargaining table, the parties arrange the seating in a U-shape just as they did during the training process. They also may use an "empty chair" technique if many people are involved. A few principals sit at the table permanently, but both the company and union designate empty chairs for other people to use when they want to participate in discussions. Alternative styles allow for nonbinding discussion during brainstorming so that people are able to be creative. People do not take copious notes during the negotiations. Flip charts are used as memory joggers and reflect the facts, the interests, or the solution to a problem. The parties acknowledge the importance of the charts and display them on the walls during the entire negotiating process.

The Nature of the Ongoing Negotiations

In *adversarial negotiations,* the ongoing bargaining is confrontational and very party-line. Negotiators are very careful not to say anything that contradicts their constituencies' demands. Rather than participating in a dialogue with one another, the spokespeople deliver what can be characterized as sequential monologues. Good listening skills are not considered a strength because scarcely anything the other party says actually reflects what they intend. Very little is accomplished during the ongoing negotiations.

To illustrate this frustration with the ongoing negotiation, one union spokesperson placed a large box on the negotiating table several weeks after negotiations had begun. The box shook and noises came from inside. Finally the company negotiator asked the union representative why he had brought the box.

The union negotiator answered that he had learned it was the company spokesperson's birthday and this was his present. Quite surprised, the company spokesperson opened his gift to find a hamster in a cage on its running wheel. After saying thank you, the company negotiator asked why the union representative had chosen this present. The union spokesperson replied, "It is just like our negotiations. We are running very fast in circles and getting nowhere."

In *mutual gains negotiations,* the parties work together in a problem-solving approach. The dialogue has far more openness and candor. At times, people are out of character during the nonbinding brainstorming processes. They generate some ideas that would not only serve their own interests but benefit the other side's interests. They do this because they know that what they say in the brainstorming process is not binding and the ideas may be helpful in generating effective 18th camel solutions to problems they are addressing.

Documentation and Language

In *adversarial negotiations,* the parties are held accountable for the notes taken during the process. The parties take turns recording what is said. After each day of negotiations, the side that did not take the notes reviews the other side's notes and signs off on each page. By signing off, the reviewing party agrees that the notes accurately reflect what the parties stated. The reviewing party references contradictory statements.

The specific contract language is often not written until after the bargaining process concludes. In most union-management negotiations, management writes the language. Not surprisingly, on occasion it varies slightly from what was actually agreed to. In one case, for example, a company representative who wrote an agreement did not think the company negotiators wanted the word "must" to appear in a contract, so he unilaterally substituted the word "may." It was only a one-word change, but it was viewed by the union as a betrayal of their trust—they had assumed the company would write the contract just as they had agreed to it.

In adversarial negotiations, mediators are brought in to avoid an impasse. They sometimes close a deal by using ambiguous language in an article so that both sides think they have won. In the meantime, the employees get back to work, assuming that time, the parties, the grievance process, and the arbitrators will ultimately work out the right answer. Invariably, this becomes an issue in the next negotiation process and perpetuates the adversarial climate.

In *mutual gains negotiations,* flip charts are used as memory joggers. As the negotiations proceed, parties develop framework agreements. This means that the parties identify key phrases on flip charts or electronically, and if any specific variables still need to be negotiated, a blank is left and those variables are negotiated at another time. Every issue that is negotiated appears on flip charts displayed in front of the parties so that throughout the process they can see the issues that are agreed upon. Language then is written almost as the negotiations proceed—not in the specific "wordsmith" sense, but in the sense that the general points are actually agreed to on the flip charts.

A union representative joins the company in writing the final language for the contract. Both sides recognize that the language determines how the union membership and the senior executives of the company see the agreement. Although the company takes the lead in actually writing the contract, the union representative ensures that it reflects the intent of the agreement that was reached.

The Method of Reaching Agreement

In *adversarial negotiations,* the negotiations usually take several months using the power approach and very little is accomplished. People posture and use subtle deceptiveness so the other party will accept their position. Invariably, at the "11th hour" (a term used to denote the last few days or hours of negotiations) spokespeople finally begin to use the interest approach. Over a drink or through telephone conversations, they say they have to get down to business and make a deal.

At the conclusion of the negotiations, only the major issues are examined because there is not enough time to deal with all the issues during the negotiations. To avoid a strike or lockout, veiled threats are made so that one side will compromise and the parties can reach a solution. Often, negotiating occurs at the last minute, but it is often too little and too late. An agreement is reached and concessions are made, but trust has been destroyed. Ultimately, many are dissatisfied with the agreement even though it may be ratified. Throughout the duration of the agreement, parties attempt to get even and repay the injustices they feel they suffered because of the way the contract was negotiated.

In *mutual gains negotiations,* the bargaining is very tough but focuses on exploring common interests and achieving mutual gains solutions. The parties investigate all mechanisms openly and honestly to try to reach resolutions that benefit everyone. A solution that is good enough for today is good enough for tomorrow. This means that if the parties consider a solution, they study the risks and benefits to see whether that solution will withstand intense scrutiny. When solutions are reached, the parties feel a sense of commitment to an agreement that they are able to make and to put into operation. In mutual gains negotiations, the deal is the beginning rather than the end of the process.

At the conclusion of the process, each party independently reflects on the contract and ensures that the mutual gains contract is at least as good as what would have resulted from a rights or power approach. The parties then sign a memorandum. The constituencies see a document that reflects a contract between the union and the company just as they do when the negotiations are adversarial. However, the contract is shorter, it is written more clearly, and the ideas are far more inventive and appropriate to the situations.

The constituencies who are not negotiating are more concerned about the outcome of the negotiation than they are with the process. If the solution is wise and simple so that everyone can understand it and live by it and if it is one that fosters ongoing negotiations, the mutual gains agreement will achieve success—for the negotiators, the company, and the people who work with it after the contract is signed.

When these parties use adversarial negotiations, the parties identify all the demands independently and secretly. The creativity and thought process happen separately for both parties. When the two parties use mutual gains negotiating, they engage in joint problem solving, are trustworthy and honest with each other, and discover better solutions to the problems they have. It actually helps the parties expand their "pie." In contrast, if one of the parties generates a solution independently and tells the other party what the demand is, the parties then have to negotiate how to divide the pie.

The 18th camel is available if people are willing to seek it out. If parties understand what the problems are, they can resolve those problems. It requires trust. Both sides can take comfort that if they choose to trust a little, they have not given up their power. They can always use their power as a last resort. By engaging in mutual gains negotiations, they do not lose their power. Instead, they put their power in reserve and first try to solve the pressing issues both sides face.

SUMMARY

- An essential ability needed to achieve union-management peace is skill in mutual gains negotiating and problem solving.

- Adversarial and mutual gains negotiations are similar in that they both involve the same approaches to negotiating—interests, rights, and power. However, mutual gains and adversarial negotiation styles differ dramatically in how and when interests, rights, and power are used.

- To achieve mutual gains, negotiators are guided by three core principles for successful negotiating:

- Develop wise solutions.
- Identify the simplest possible solutions.
- Enhance the quality of the relationship between the parties.

- Never reach an agreement your first-line supervisors and stewards cannot implement.

- The preferred method in mutual gains negotiations is to resolve conflicts using an interest approach without having to resort to a rights approach. Nevertheless, there are times when rights are necessary and even desirable as an effective buffer from the immediate application of power.

- The collective labor agreement is useful and essential to support the mutual gains negotiations agreement between the company and its unions.

- Power is much more effective before it's used than after.

- Power is rare in the mutual gains environment. It is much more common within the adversarial negotiating arena.

- Parties do not give up power in mutual gains negotiation; they use it only as a last resort.

- One of the biggest challenges mutual gains negotiators face is to determine when the interest approach is not working and, therefore, when to use the rights and power approaches. In addition, if rights and power have to be used, negotiators must make sure these approaches do not sabotage mutual gains negotiations for the next problem they encounter.

- In adversarial negotiations, training for the two parties to the dispute is done separately. In mutual gains negotiations, the two parties train jointly, which is often nonbinding.

- In adversarial negotiations, parties often survey the people they represent to determine the demands they want to make. In mutual gains negotiating, they survey their constituencies to discover the problems needing resolution.

- In adversarial negotiations, parties prepare extensively prior to negotiations to put together formal demands. In mutual gains negotiations, both parties present their hope for the success of the negotiation process and present what they think should be the ground rules (principles for proceeding) for the negotiations. They then identify the agenda of problems.

- In adversarial negotiations, the parties sit on opposite sides of a rectangular table. In mutual gains negotiations, the seating arrangements are often very informal.

- In adversarial negotiations, the ongoing dialogue is confrontational and very party-line. In mutual gains negotiations, the parties work together in a problem-solving approach.

- In adversarial negotiations, the parties are held accountable for the notes that are taken during the process. In mutual gains negotiations, flip charts are used as memory joggers.

- In adversarial negotiations, the negotiations usually take several months using the power approach and the parties accomplish very little. In mutual gains bargaining, the negotiations are very tough but focus on exploring common interests and achieving mutual gains solutions.

CHAPTER 3

The Paradox of Trust and Mistrust

If you make vacation arrangements at a luxurious resort and arrive at your destination only to be told by the airline that your luggage is lost, you will probably be:

1. Disappointed,

2. Furious, or

3. Disappointed and furious.

Because of the airline's mistake, you may spend valuable vacation time communicating with the airline about when your luggage will arrive, washing out the clothes you have on, and shopping for new items. What happens if the airline does not respond to your predicament? Will you tell the airline how you feel? Usually, dissatisfied customers tell approximately 20 people about their frustration with a company but often do not discuss it with the company itself. Frequently, the company doesn't know the customer is making negative comments about them.

Trust can be very fragile in a business context. After a shareholder takeover, for example, the displaced party often waits for the opportunity to retaliate. If a time comes when power is redistributed, the disadvantaged party will engage in "terrorist" activities to inflict pain on the perpetrator of the crime.

"Terrorism" is often viewed as an activity that needs to be obliterated. In union-management disputes, terrorist acts can be aggressive responses to the other side's overuse of power. The only recourse for the powerless is to find an alternative "terrorist" method to even the power base. A well-known principle in negotiating is that one should never "win too big" or the opposition will focus on getting even by any method it can find.

Powerless countries also find ways to strike back at their adversaries. In the recent Gulf War, Iraq recognized that it could not fight the United States-led alliance. Instead, it conducted a brilliant military maneuver; it chose not to fight back—to become defenseless. The U.S.-led alliance had no choice but to stop the aggression before it completed its unstated mission of changing the Baghdad leadership.

Shortly after a cease-fire agreement was reached, Iraq demonstrated it was fully capable of fighting by attacking the Kurds. Iraq's nonviolent response to the U.S.-led alliance was strictly a military ploy that worked exceedingly well. We can only imagine the extent to which Iraq will direct terrorist activities against the U.S.-led alliance countries in response to its humiliation.

A union leader pointed out that Iraq's strategy demonstrated its understanding of the "wolf-pack syndrome." When wolves are totally helpless, they lie on their backs with their paws in the air, placing themselves at the mercy of others. The wolves in power usually refrain from destroying them. Wolves that have displayed weakness once are not necessarily weak forever. Similarly, if negotiators trust once and are abused, they may not be willing to trust again.

WINNING ISN'T FINAL; LOSING ISN'T FATAL

Expect that if you hurt someone while you are in a position of strength, that person will find an opportunity to hurt you in return. It is very possible that you will not be strong forever and that the person you hurt will reciprocate. People rarely forget feeling betrayed or being hurt when they are weak. As one negotiator said, "What goes around, comes around." When an opponent has a moment of weakness, the strong negotiator recognizes the opportunity to work out a fair deal—not one that takes advantage of the counterpart's weaknesses.

Dissatisfied parties who have been given no choice often find ways of retaliating through terrorism. In one negotiation, the union demanded a $4 per hour wage increase. The company responded by saying it would take a strike over the issue. The strike lasted for six months, and in the interim, the market share and the customer base of the company eroded dramatically. The union returned to work without the $4 increase. However, the company found that costs rose by the equivalent of $4 per hour per person as a result of inefficiencies the employees introduced.

THE PARADOX OF TRUST AND MISTRUST[11]

Think of trust as a precious jewel. You keep it inside a beautiful case, polish it frequently, and treasure it. The tiniest scratch on this jewel can destroy its value, and it will be very difficult to regain that value once again. Just as you would care for a precious jewel that is your most treasured possession, you must nurture your relationships so that you develop trust. It is a paradox that trust is vulnerable even to the slightest betrayal. A lie, a break of confidence, a bit of withheld information, or a personal attack—any of these can result in an immediate break of trust.

Ironically, the mistrust that is created from a brief moment persists. A party's attempts to regain that trust are often held suspect by the other party and assumed to reflect manipulative behavior and therefore not be trustworthy.

The Paradox of Trust and Mistrust:
Trust Takes Forever to Build and a Moment to Destroy,
While Mistrust Takes Forever to Destroy
and a Moment to Build

TRUST AND MUTUAL GAINS NEGOTIATIONS

The foundation of mutual gains negotiations is the extent to which trust is built between the negotiating parties. Unfortunately, mistrust is difficult to destroy, while it takes only a moment of indiscretion to eliminate trust. All relationships are built on some level of trust. To develop that trust, parties must deliver what is expected of them and maximize the relationship.

The level of trust between parties is usually reflected in the text of the collective bargaining agreement. It is evident by the number of letters of understanding that follow a signature page and the attention to exceptions within the agreement. As indicated earlier, you never make a peace treaty between friends. You have a collective agreement because parties often have limited trust between them. The collective agreement creates boundaries. The greater the opportunity to maximize that trust through living the agreement, the greater the ability to negotiate wise solutions that are simple enough to live by and that enhance the quality of the relationships.

Trust does not occur by accident. It results from building assumptions and expectations that are supported by actual behavior. The behaviors are continually reinforced so that all parties' needs are met.

Assumption of Mistrust or Trust

The assumption of trust or mistrust is based on relationships. People believe they can trust you during and after the negotiation process based on factors such as what people are saying, what they know about you from previous experiences, and what rumors they have heard about you.

People also have very important personal characteristics that determine whether they are trusting by nature. Some people are immediately trusting as soon as that trust is deserved, while others remain mistrustful. And there are those who trust even when situations are not worthy of trust.

The adversarial negotiating process, by virtue of its hostile environment and relationships, engenders mistrust. In addition, people selected to negotiate often have personal characteristics that make them cynical and mistrustful. These characteristics are useful in adversarial negotiations, but are a hurdle in the process of mutual gains negotiations. To break out of that mistrust, both parties in a negotiation must be willing to see the potential of union-management peace and make the effort to create it.

Expectations of Trust or Mistrust

People's trust or mistrust leads them to specific expectations of future behaviors. Most people perform to expectations rather than potential. While some individuals are driven to fulfill their potential, expectations are more likely to be the driving force for performance. The idea of creating objectives as a stimulus to help people increase their performance is built on this concept.

Here's an exercise that demonstrates the power of expectations: A pad-board sheet of paper is placed eight feet off the ground. With both feet on the ground, participants reach as high as they can and draw a line across the pad board. Most people are able to do this reasonably well. Next, the same people are asked to try the exercise again. This time they are requested to draw the line at least two inches above the first line they drew. In most cases the participants can do this.

This exercise is intriguing because the participants have two inches to spare the first time even though they are asked to draw the line as high as they can. The first time they draw a line, they are exploring their potential. But when they are asked to draw a line two inches above the first line, they are responding to expectations. Performance attributed to meeting expectations often exceeds performance based on fulfilling potential.

The message of this exercise is the power of expectations. Expectations govern much of our lives, shape the way we approach situations, and have tremendous impact on trust.

The expectation of trust or mistrust contributes to a person's willingness to participate in mutual gains negotiations. Specific strategies are needed to maximize negotiators' potential to trust each other, and great care should be taken to make sure the trust is not betrayed.

Behavior That Is Trustworthy or Not Trustworthy

Behaviors do not occur until someone forms expectations of trust or mistrust. An individual's behaviors toward another are often reciprocated. Negotiators can assume that their counterparts will probably respond to their displays of trust or mistrust in like manner.

During the process of negotiating, a roller coaster of trust or mistrust emerges. If the process is one of continual mistrust between participants and their behaviors support that mistrust, the participants begin to expect each other to be untrustworthy. The negotiation process breaks down, collaborative work becomes nonexistent, and the ability to reach mutual gains solutions is limited. Both parties lose in this case. If one of the parties emerges as an apparent winner—even in the short term—the loser usually retaliates with a "terrorist" attack at the winner if the opportunity presents itself.

The Three Levels of Trust

Let's consider an example of trust in a totally different environment. Say you are having Sunday brunch and need to purchase some bagels. At the bagel store, you ask for a dozen bagels, but the salesperson gives you only 11. You gently explain that you asked for 12 and received 11. The salesperson insists she gave you 12 and suggests that you must have eaten one. You begin to get angry and ask for the manager. Unfortunately, the salesperson says she is the manager and the owner of the store.

Later, another bagel store opens down the block. You begin purchasing bagels there and tell everyone you meet about the terrible customer service at the first bagel store. The owner at that store failed to understand a basic principle about building trust: Meet your customer's expectations to achieve a basic level of satisfaction—or the customer will go elsewhere.

Now, let's say more and more bagel stores open on the same street and it becomes known as "bagel street." The store where you buy your bagels begins to give a "baker's dozen," or 13 bagels, one extra with each dozen purchased. You are delighted with the bonus you are receiving and continue to give that store your business.

The owner of the store decides to shock her customers into permanent customer loyalty. When you order a dozen bagels, she gives you three dozen. Since you don't need that many bagels and your freezer is too small to store them, the bagels will be wasted. You don't understand why the store owner gave you so many. You even wonder whether they were meant for someone else—maybe the store owner will accuse you of stealing the bagels. Because you had such an uncomfortable experience when you questioned the owner of the first bagel store, you decide not to question the second one. Your concern convinces you to try a third bagel store down the street.

The second store owner tried to build trust by exceeding your expectations. But by surpassing your expectations excessively, the strategy backfired and actually reduced your loyalty and satisfaction. The moral for the second store owner is: If you are one step ahead, you are a genius, but if you are two steps ahead, you are a quack. Exceed expectations to build trust, but don't exceed them by so much that the other party does not understand what happened.

Now, back to your bagel adventure. You still need bagels for your Sunday brunches, so you start purchasing your bagels at a third bagel store. They are also giving bakers' dozens when you order 12 bagels. You are delighted that they exceed your expectations in a way you can comprehend. One Saturday afternoon you are very busy and realize you may not get to the bagel store before it closes at 7:00 P.M.—one hour after all the other bagel stores close. You race to the store and arrive just five minutes before closing time. However, you find that all the bagel shelves have been cleaned out. With your head down, you slowly walk out the door. As you reach your car, the store owner runs after you and says, "Hello! It's good to see you. I knew you would come, so I put aside a dozen bagels just for you."

You are in shock! At the precise moment of your vulnerability, you are rescued. The store owner not only exceeds your expectations for the delivery of good-quality bagels but surpasses expectations on the trust side as well. The store is there for you when you need it. Even if other stores start undercutting this store on price, your loyalty will not be shaken—they will have a customer as long as the trust continues to exist.

The bagel story is a simple way of illustrating the levels of trust that can be reached in negotiations as well. The two essential variables of building trust or mistrust are:

- Expectations
- Behavior

Mistrust is created when your behavior does not meet the other party's expectations.

Behavior that does not meet expectations = MISTRUST

An acceptable level of trust exists when you behave in a way that is consistent with the other party's expectations of you.

Behavior that meets expectations = ACCEPTABLE LEVEL OF TRUST

Behavior consistent with the other party's expectations may allow you to achieve an acceptable level of trust, but if you exceed expectations the trust has greater sustaining power.

> Behavior that exceeds expectations = SUSTAINED TRUST

Added to the two variables, expectations and behavior, is the highest level of trust, which includes the supportive relationship between the parties. If parties have established a supportive relationship, they will be able to help each other in time of need. They are loyal to their counterparts and ensure that they do not do anything that will hurt their credibility with their constituencies. They are also able to recover more quickly if they ever need to resort to power as a last resort.

They engage in mutual gains negotiations at a level of "loyal trust," which helps them achieve union-management peace.

> Behavior that exceeds expectations + a supportive relationship
> = LOYAL TRUST

The Three Stages of Building a Supportive Relationship

A supportive relationship essential for loyal trust is characterized by three stages. Each stage creates a trusting relationship that is deeper and more lasting than the previous. The stages are:

Stage 1—Trust in your competence.

Stage 2—Trust in your honesty.

Stage 3—Trust that when I am vulnerable you will not hurt me and that you will be there for me.

Imagine that you are asked by two colleagues to participate in an experiment in which you will have to demonstrate a significant amount of trust. They ask you to allow them to take care of you when they take you to a restaurant—blindfolded. To participate in this exercise, you need a loyal trust relationship with your colleagues (behavior that exceeds expectations + a supportive relationship). The minimum standards for a supportive relationship are Stages 1 and 2. You must trust their competence and honesty.

You first assess your colleagues' competence to care for you through lunch. You consider whether they are able to perform the task and whether they will tell you if a particular task is beyond their capability. You decide you can trust that they will fulfill the first stage of a supportive relationship: the basic competence to do the task.

You then consider the second stage of a supportive relationship. Your colleagues may have the competence, but will they do what they say they will do? Will they not only "walk the talk" but also "walk the talk of quality thought"? Do you trust their honesty when they say they will take you to lunch? Assume you feel sufficiently reassured that your colleagues will do as they promised, so you proceed with the exercise.

Now, let's say your colleagues take you to a restaurant with stairs to the entrance. Instead of instructing you about the stairs and carefully leading you up them, they don't tell you about them. You stumble on the first step. They catch you, but then take you up the stairs very quickly without any regard for the fact that you are blindfolded. You have no idea how many steps are remaining and are nervous because you have just recovered from a slip on one of the steps. You begin to doubt their level of competence and honesty. They are not doing what they said they would do. You may decide to take off the blindfold and stop the exercise.

Instead, imagine that your colleagues instruct you adequately about the stairs and lead you carefully and slowly up them so that you do not stumble. They have maintained Stage 1 (competence) and Stage 2 (honesty) trust. While you are still very anxious, you have a basic level of trust in them and are looking forward to relaxing and enjoying your food. You begin to ask yourself whether you can extend trust to the third stage of a supportive relationship.

Your colleagues lead you to your table and give you very explicit instructions about where you are and how to be seated and then make certain you are seated without any problems. After you are seated, you overhear someone laughing and talking about your blindfold. Your colleagues come to your defense and explain what you are doing. As a result, the other people express amazement at your courage in participating in the exercise. Next, your colleagues talk to you about how the table is set so that you know exactly where your plate, silverware, and glass are positioned. They suggest that you order something that will be easy for you to eat blindfolded.

You begin to realize that your colleagues may be trustworthy at the third stage of a supportive relationship. They are serious about being there for you at every turn. You feel that you can trust your colleagues completely because they have demonstrated their loyalty to you. You relax and enjoy the meal.

HOW TO BECOME MORE TRUSTWORTHY IN NEGOTIATIONS

At a minimum, parties in mutual gains negotiations should strive to build a trust relationship by meeting expectations and by achieving the first two stages of a supportive relationship. They need to know their areas of competence and communicate honestly. This means that each party will trust the other to deliver the expectations that have been created. Trust allows the negotiating parties to communicate honestly about their problems and to explore mutual gains solutions jointly. Trust allows you to understand alternatives and make effective choices.

Most people find that Stage 3 of a supportive relationship applies only to a love relationship. Many people who are divorced find the relationship has ended because Stage 3 was broken. Somehow at the moment of greatest need, one of the two parties breaks the trust and is not there for the other partner when needed the most.

If negotiating parties are able to develop a Stage 3 support-ive relationship, they will probably achieve magnificent results—far beyond their anticipation. In Stage 3, parties have a joint understanding that they will use the interests approach for the mutual gains negotiations process and that they will apply rights and power approaches only as a last resort.

HOW TO MOVE FROM MISTRUST TO TRUST

When you lose the trust of the other party, you must try to regain it very quickly. Mistrust that lingers builds in strength and be-comes much more difficult to overcome. As soon as you see mistrust emerging, respond immediately.

You may fall out of trust when the other person begins to mistrust you based on:

1. Expectations: A perception that is incorrect because of a misunderstanding, or,

2. Behavior: An inappropriate action on your part.

When other parties mistrust you based on a misunderstand-ing, your chances of persuading them to trust you are directly related to your relationship with them. If the trust relationship is strong and loyal, they will probably believe you, give you a chance to explain your interpretation of events, and then consider rebuilding the trust. If you do not have a strong, loyal trust relationship, they may see your attempts to defend yourself as a defensive reaction. This will only enhance the perception of mistrust they may already have of you.

If you have a strong relationship with your counterpart and have been misjudged, this misjudgment may occur for two reasons:

- **The behaviors the other party believed you showed are less than what you know you actually delivered.** You will then need to clarify that you actually did what was expected of you.

- **You and your counterpart differ in your assessments of what is expected of you.** In this case, if you have a strong relationship, you may be able to clarify the expectations, renegotiate them, and show that you are doing what your counterpart expects of you. In a situation like this, the problems often are communication based. If you act quickly, you probably will be able to reduce the mistrust and regain the trust. If you let the mistrust linger and allow your counterpart to believe that you are not delivering the agreed-upon expectations, your good relationship can be destroyed.

Of course, sometimes you deserve to fall out of trust. This is because you either do not behave in a manner consistent with what is expected of you or you agree to expectations that are beyond your ability to deliver. In these situations, the following actions are essential:

- Respond quickly.
- Help the other party understand that your behavior will match expectations in the future.
- Establish an agreement about expectations you believe you can fulfill.
- Maximize your strong relationship if it exists. The better the trust relationship, the more likely you will recover from the mistrust.

Give a Free Stage 3 Trust: Be There for Them When They Are Vulnerable

The quickest way to recover from mistrust is to be there for your counterparts at the moment of their greatest need—to give them a free "Stage 3" level of trust. If you help rather than hurt your counterparts when they are vulnerable, you can improve their trust significantly, and they may believe that you are willing to change. The gift of trust becomes a dividend that will be available to you in any future negotiation.

One poignant example of this occurred in a recent negotiation. In a premeeting between the chief spokespeople for the company and union, the union representative accidentally left behind the folder that included his demands for the upcoming round of negotiations. After the meeting, the company spokesperson found the folder, looked inside at the first page, and identified it as the union demands.

The company spokesperson saw this as a no-lose, trust-building opportunity. He chose not to read the contents of the folder but instead phoned the union spokesperson. He told him that he had found the folder, looked at the first page, noticed what it was, closed the folder, and called him immediately.

If the company spokesperson had looked at the contents of the folder or photocopied them, he would have been in a vulnerable position. Later he might have slipped and revealed something he saw in the document, proving that he was lying about not having looked at the material. In addition, the union spokesperson would present the demands the next week, so there was little advantage in knowing the explicit demands early. Finally, leaving the folder might have been an actual setup—to see if the company spokesperson could be trusted enough to engage in mutual gains negotiations.

The union negotiator's response was very astute. He recognized an opportunity to clean the slate on the trust extended to him. Instead of saying that the company person should send the material to him, the union negotiator told him to shred it! It was a brilliant move in the chess game of escalating trust. Clearly, if the trust account was not balanced right away, the union representative would "owe him one" measure of trust sometime during the negotiation. So the union representative paid it back by trusting him to shred the material.

The company person told the union representative to hold the line while he shredded the folder. He put the phone down, shredded the material, and returned to the phone to tell him it was finished. They thanked each other and hung up the phone.

Later, the company spokesperson said he wished he had saved the shredded paper. He thought it might have been beneficial sometime later in the negotiations as a symbolic statement of trust. Nevertheless, the actions he took developed the trust of the union representative sufficiently so that he was willing to start exploring some level of mutual gains negotiations with the company.

BE CONSISTENT OVER THE LONG RUN

The best way to build trust, although it takes much longer, is to change your behavior and start exceeding expectations. Changing mistrust to trust by just promising to be better and by trying to fight your counterpart's expectations with your expectations usually results in disbelief. The other party assumes you are lying. He or she may not believe you, assuming that since you did not deliver before, you will not deliver now. If you change your behavior, however, and sustain it over an extended period of time, your counterpart may begin to believe you. Once your actions show that you have made a change, then you can explain your new expectations.

Think of trust levels as the floors in a 10-story building, with the 10th floor being the highest level of trust. You can proceed with mutual gains negotiations if you are on the second floor; however, you will have to work slowly and focus more on the problems that are in the common interest. By doing this, you can demonstrate mutual gains and begin to climb to higher floors.

It is extremely rare that any two parties will reach the highest floor. That extent of trust is reserved for parties who have very few or no separate interests. The parties in a negotiation will always have separate interests, focusing on how to represent their constituencies' interests fairly. The two negotiating parties never really become one team. They are two teams with some common interests on which to build mutual gains solutions. But if they can climb to the seventh floor, or even the fifth, they will have a significant opportunity to reshape the way the company and the union work together for the betterment of all.

TRUST AND AGREEMENT

Empirical evidence indicates that the stronger the trust between negotiating parties, the greater the probability the parties will discover solutions that will result in mutual gains agreements. Nevertheless, low trust doesn't guarantee disagreement, just as high trust doesn't guarantee agreement.

When trust is low, disagreement often results because of the destructive nature of the interactions in which the parties treat one another with personal contempt. The negotiations show a focus on self-interest, a low level of innovation and risk taking, and inadequate resolution of problems. A disagreement on one issue probably will affect the way the next issue will be resolved. It may be difficult for these negotiating parties to reach agreement. However, low-trust relationships can still generate agreements for a variety of reasons. These include:

- The solution is obvious, and even though trust is low, the parties can agree on a common direction.
- The parties have a common enemy that unites them. (For example, trust may be low between a company and union, but they will work together to resist a common problem such as being shut down.)
- An unequal distribution of power requires one of the parties to agree passively to a solution. This party will "get even" when the opportunity arises.

When trust is high, disagreements are often constructive and issue based. There may be conflict, but it is without contempt. If the parties cannot agree on an issue, it does not mean they will be unable to agree on the next issue.

When negotiating parties agree to a common direction and have a high-trust relationship, they often are willing to engage in innovative problem solving and some risk taking. The parties consider the common interests and discover creative solutions they can put into operation. High-trust agreements are longer lasting and create momentum for resolving more complex problems.

The return on investment for building trust between union and management is substantial. The collective agreements developed when trust is high are designed to achieve mutual gains. The trust relationship contributes to meaningful continuous dialogue between the parties even after contract negotiations. The climate necessary to get *beyond the walls of conflict* is in place.

SUMMARY

- In union-management disputes, terrorist acts can be aggressive responses to the overuse of power by the other side.

- A well-known principle in negotiating is that one should never "win too big" or the opposition will focus on getting even by any method it can find.

- Trust takes forever to build and a moment to destroy, while mistrust takes forever to destroy and a moment to build.

- The foundation of mutual gains negotiations is the extent to which trust is built between the negotiating parties.

- The adversarial negotiating process, by virtue of its hostile environment and relationships, engenders mistrust.

- The trust or mistrust individuals possess leads them to specific expectations of future behaviors.

- Most people perform to expectations rather than to potential.

- The expectation of trust or mistrust contributes to a person's willingness to participate in mutual gains negotiations. Specific strategies are necessary to maximize negotiators' potential to trust each other, and great care should be taken to make sure the trust is not betrayed.

- Negotiators can assume that their counterparts will probably respond to their displays of trust or mistrust in like manner.

- The two essential variables of building trust or mistrust are behavior and expectations.
  - Behavior that does not meet expectations = MISTRUST.
  - Behavior that meets expectations = ACCEPTABLE LEVEL OF TRUST.
  - Behavior that exceeds expectations = SUSTAINED TRUST.
  - Behavior that exceeds expectations + a supportive relationship = LOYAL TRUST.

- A supportive relationship essential for loyal trust is characterized by three stages. Each stage creates a trusting relationship that is deeper and more lasting than the previous. The stages are:
  - Stage 1—Trust in your competence.
  - Stage 2—Trust in your honesty.
  - Stage 3—Trust that when I am vulnerable you will not hurt me and that you will be there for me.

- At a minimum, parties in mutual gains negotiations should strive to build a trust relationship by meeting expectations and by achieving the first two stages (competence and honesty) of a supportive relationship.

- When you lose the trust of the other party, you must try to regain it very quickly.

- You may fall out of trust when the other person begins to mistrust you based on:

1. Expectation: A perception that is incorrect because of a misunderstanding, or,

2. Behavior: An inappropriate action on your part.

- When other parties mistrust you based on a misunderstanding, your chances of persuading them to trust you are directly related to your relationship with them.

- The quickest way to recover from mistrust is to be there for your counterparts at the moment of their greatest need—to give them a free "Stage 3" level of trust.

- Empirical evidence indicates that the stronger the trust between negotiating parties, the greater the probability they will discover solutions to their problems that will result in mutual gains agreements.

- High-trust agreements are longer lasting and create momentum for resolving more complex problems.

Planning for Successful Negotiations

Mutual gains negotiating consists of five phases. Figure 4–1 illustrates the circular and repetitive nature of the five phases.

FIGURE 4–1

The Cycle of Mutual Gains Negotiations

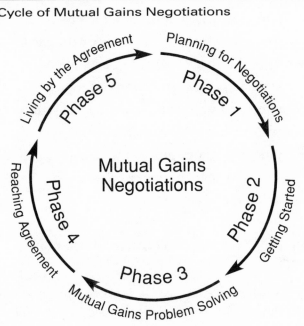

I will address the first of these phases, Planning, in this chapter. The next four chapters explore Phases 2 through 5 in greater depth. The five phases are:

Phase 1—Planning (Chapter 4).

Phase 2—Getting Started with Face-to-Face Negotiations (Chapter 5).

Phase 3—Mutual Gains Problem Solving (Chapters 6 and 7).

Phase 4—Reaching Agreement (Chapter 8).

Phase 5—Living by the Agreement (Chapter 8).

To achieve union-management peace through mutual gains negotiating, Planning (Phase 1) is essential. Each of the parties separately reflects, plans, and explores possibilities. They consider both their negotiating team and those representatives outside the negotiator groups who will have strong opinions about how the negotiations are proceeding.

The planning process has several crucial features:

- Identifying the negotiating team members.
- Mutual commitments within a negotiating team.
- The role of the "back room" in negotiations.
- The role of a "parallel planning committee."
- Joint union-management negotiation training.
- Conducting internal and external surveys.
- Presenting issues for approval to negotiate.
- Simulating the negotiations process during planning.
- Completing the planning phase.

IDENTIFYING THE NEGOTIATING TEAM MEMBERS

In a simple negotiation, the people involved in negotiating are at the negotiating table. The number of people who take part in more elaborate negotiations may be much higher, and many may not be at the negotiation table. This section describes the selection and roles of those involved in a very large negotiation. To identify the resources needed for smaller negotiations that require fewer personnel, scale back as necessary.

Selection and Roles of the Mutual Gains Negotiators

The negotiating team you select sends an important message to your counterparts. A team of professional negotiators, who will not have to work with the contract after it is completed, may be viewed as aggressive and adversarial by their counterparts. Negotiators who are "line" employees of the company (i.e., members of the union or of management) send a different message. Your counterparts will assume that these individuals have a greater desire to collaborate because they will have to live with each other and their agreement after they complete the contract.

A fundamental principle of mutual gains negotiating is that you never negotiate an agreement that will upset your frontline supervisor or steward group. People who will have to uphold an agreement should be appointed to a negotiating team. They are the point of contact, the people who have to administer the agreement. If they are part of the negotiations, their needs will probably be satisfied.

The negotiating team should have some professional negotiators, but the majority should be the managers or employees within the union or the company. This establishes negotiating expertise on the team as well as grass-roots knowledge and experience.

Perhaps the most important person on a negotiating team is the chief spokesperson. This individual leads the process, including the internal negotiations and those with counterparts. A spokesperson should be well spoken, know the business, and be patient and not abrasive.

The chief spokesperson should also have the right to make decisions. Otherwise, the negotiations will lose momentum because the spokesperson has to call decision makers outside the negotiating room for all the decisions that must be made.

The chief spokesperson also has a major role either in determining who will be part of the negotiating team or in appointing team members to specific roles. On the company side, the spokesperson may be able to appoint people to the team. On the union side, the senior elected representatives are often automatically on the negotiating team. The spokesperson can help appoint people to roles in which they will have the greatest impact.

MUTUAL COMMITMENTS WITHIN A NEGOTIATING TEAM

In the planning process, the negotiating team makes commitments about how the members will work together during the negotiations. Four examples of commitments teams have made in actual negotiations are presented below. Each has its own flavor and may be useful if you are considering generating these kinds of commitments among your team members.

Example One: The Trust Agreement

In one negotiation planning process, eight chief negotiators were attempting to negotiate eight tables simultaneously. They needed to develop a bond of trust to ensure that groups would not establish precedents that would force other groups to accept something inappropriate for their situations. The negotiators produced laminated cards containing the "Principles of Negotiation," and each carried a card in his or her wallet. It read as follows:

AS A MEMBER OF THE NEGOTIATING TEAM:

I TRUST that we are all competent.
I TRUST that we are all honest.
I TRUST that you will not hurt me when I make myself
vulnerable.
I TRUST that you will be there for me.
I TRUST that you will be receptive to my ideas.
I TRUST that you will not manipulate me.
I TRUST that integrity is prime for all.
I TRUST that we will communicate every solution likely to hit
the table.

. . . I TRUST YOU

They discussed the importance trust plays in negotiations. These negotiators made trust their top priority from the outset.

Example Two: Negotiating Guiding Principles

In another negotiations planning process, one group emerged with the following guiding principles for their own team. They duplicated these principles and placed them in their planning room to help guide them to a successful mutual gains resolution of their contract negotiations. Their principles were as follows:

- **Even the most difficult situations can be revitalized by trying to rebuild trust.** Trust begets trust. Keep questioning your paradigms. Keep asking yourself what the underlying motivators are in order to find the mutual gains solutions. Never say no before you hear what the other person says. If it seems simple and the problem is not getting resolved, you probably are missing another motivator.

- **Always step back and look at the process.** Don't get too close to things and lose perspective. Depend on others who are not at the negotiating table to help you review what has happened and to think through the next steps to reach a mutual gains solution. Make sure you keep your collective memory so that nothing disappears and you can understand the nuances of the negotiation process.

- **Always maintain your integrity.** In negotiations, that's probably all you have. It is something that once lost can never be found. Be true to yourself and focus on your mind-set. Essentially, you need to know where you are and where you need to be at the end of the negotiations. You do not need a predetermined presentation. Solicit support on the process and acknowledge the competence and contribution of the other side so they will continually give input and you will be able to work together.

- **When you are challenged, let go.** If you are wrong, acknowledge your mistake and say, "Obviously, I'm going down the wrong track, and maybe you can help me figure out which way to go."

- **Always know the knowable.** If people have competence in an area, acknowledge their competence. You should have an in-depth understanding of the pertinent contract and background information.

- **Always deal with the forest before you deal with the trees, and then the trees before you get into the bark.** To make sure you establish intent, restrain yourself from focusing on the details too soon. As the world continues to become more complex, intent and values will govern union-management relations just as people will be expected to communicate through continuous dialogue.

Example Three: Commitments within the Negotiating Team

In yet another negotiating situation, one of the negotiating teams developed the following detailed set of commitments to each other:

- **Personal Integrity**—Personal integrity is your internal source of power. Do what you say you will do. Stay true to yourself and what you believe in and bring your concerns to the table. The group agrees to trust each other's competence. The motto is "Do it right the first time every time."

- **Communications**—Provide clear, constructive feedback to one another. When you criticize, give a positive suggestion. Avoid personal attacks. Attack the issue, not the individual. Always be alert and open-minded. Everyone participates. Anytime and anywhere it is okay to call "time-out." Ensure maximum confidentiality.

- **Encourage Openness**—Listen to each other and be open to new and different ideas. There are no "stripes" on the bargaining unit; all have an equal say. Clear up disagreements daily. Be honest in dealing with one another. Commit to questioning the process.

- **Provide Support**—Support the team in the larger organization. Have fun at least once a day. Find mechanisms to bring down the tension. Allow people to use personal coping mechanisms flexibly. Never allow yourself to be someone other than who you are. Support someone when he or she is in distress.

- **Be Focused**—Stay focused on the negotiations and not on the noise around you. If someone suggests an idea that adds value, listen to the idea carefully and absorb it. The primary focus needs to be on the negotiations. Build in "phone time" to take care of other business.

Example Four: Commitments to a Method of Negotiating with Your Counterparts

Another negotiating team focused on the commitments to each other for their negotiations. The following are their commitments:

- **Look for the mutual gains solutions; do not lock out any alternative.** Anticipate alternatives and the fallback positions for both sides. Start with "why" you want something before you get to the specific "what" you are requesting. Present the solution as an option. Go for mutual gains solutions that are not only good today but will be good three years from now. Find mutual gains solutions that are real by sharing information openly and honestly. Do not hide possible problems; deal with them now.

- **Always give consistent messages.** Establish an expectation of your level of conduct and don't go below that no matter what the other party does. Don't say, "I'll look at it and consider it" when the answer is really "no" or when the answer is "I'll look at it but the answer will probably be no."

- **Keep asking people to differentiate between what they need and what they want and whether their wants are "pie in the sky."** Get validation that your counterpart receives things that are actually needed. You might analyze priorities as low, medium, and high and assess those differences.

- **Remember that your counterpart will not forget what you have done in the past.** Understand that if your counterpart has a problem, you have a problem.

- **Do not allow people to be attacked personally.** Do not give in to a threat. Deal with a threat and not with the issue. This applies to everyone, including the spokesperson and all the team members. Personal attacks or threats on anyone on the team are unacceptable. Warn the other side that you will leave the room if they make threats.

THE ROLE OF THE "BACK ROOM" IN NEGOTIATIONS

In larger negotiations, additional representatives are often available for specific parts of the negotiation process. For example, finance experts, pension and benefits experts, writers, and legal support representatives are frequently needed at specific times during the negotiations but do not have to be present throughout the deliberations. They are called in from time to time, and they usually work out of the "back room."

Key People in the Back Room

The back room is useful in any kind of negotiation. Essentially, a planning room is set up before negotiations that continues to exist throughout the bargaining process. The role of the people in the back room varies (if it exists at all) and may include the following:

- **Control representatives who do costing and review language during the negotiation.** One negotiator referred to this role as "measure twice and do it once." The tolerance for error of the control people in the back room is extremely low. Everyone is relying on their ability to deliver the costing and language accurately the first time.

- **People responsible for communicating and networking with their own organizations.** Back-room communications must be consistent with the negotiating parties' agreement on confidentiality and communications.

- **People responsible for debriefing the entire process
  (may occur daily or even weekly) and preparing for
  the next part of negotiations.** In this role they are the
  negotiators' sounding board. For example, after a day of
  negotiations the people at the negotiating table give
  feedback about what happened. The back-room people
  provide support and/or challenge what was done. They
  may even encourage negotiators to relax when they
  show signs of stress.

- **Subcommittees made up of people from both parties
  to help in the analysis of a problem.** The subcommittee
  members can remove some of the emotion from the
  discussion because they are not in the negotiating room
  on a regular basis.

- **People responsible for producing the notes from the
  flip charts after a problem is resolved.**

- **People who assist with tracking the negotiations,
  doing a control check, and exploring to determine if
  any major issues have been missed.** They may track
  each problem in the negotiations using a simple coding
  system. In one negotiation, the back room had a large
  chart identifying each problem and the days of
  negotiations. As the problem resolution progressed,
  they placed dots on the chart to indicate progress. A
  blue dot on a day indicated that the parties began
  discussing the problem. A yellow dot meant the problem discussion was delayed. A red dot meant the
  problem was not resolved. And a green dot meant the
  problem was successfully resolved. In a negotiation in
  which the parties trust each other, a chart like this one
  could be in the negotiations room for all parties to see.

- **People who stay in the negotiating hotel several days
  past the settlement to dot the "*i*'s" and cross the "*t*'s"
  to make sure the contract is completed successfully.**

- **People who ensure the contract is proofed and printed.**
  The rule of thumb is that "it ain't over until it's over."
  These people have a commitment to stay with the job to
  the very end.

The back room can have many valuable functions, but the
negotiating parties may interpret these functions incorrectly.
Therefore, it is important at the outset of the negotiations to
explain why the back room exists and how it adds value to the
process. Also, the back-room members should be introduced at
the beginning of the negotiations. Additional roles may become
evident as negotiations proceed.

Can the Back-Room Activities Be Done at the Negotiating Table?

In negotiations where trust is high, the company and union
representatives can perform many of the back-room functions
jointly. However, in most cases that level of collaboration requires more trust than is available. While the purpose of the
negotiations is to achieve union-management peace, the two
negotiating parties do not have to become one team.

At the end of the bargaining, the company negotiators have
to sell the agreement to their senior management, and the union
negotiators have to recommend the agreement to the union
membership for a vote. They answer to very different constituencies. In most cases they will never become one team with the
same mutual accountability.

It is preferable to acknowledge the differences between the
two teams. Time should be planned and allotted for caucuses so
that there is no unnecessary delay. During the caucuses, the
parties can work with the back room and their internal organizations to enhance the overall communication and understanding of what is taking place.

In one situation, the two parties believed that they had to
be a united team throughout the negotiations. They believed that

caucuses, even if they were planned, were inconsistent with the mutual gains negotiations approach. Toward the closing days of the negotiations, that rule became very oppressive. The parties needed to talk privately, but it seemed socially inappropriate.

Without telling each other, the parties began to resort to washroom and smoke breaks to meet their colleagues and take a few moments to plan. It set up a deceptive cycle that was totally unnecessary. They eventually talked openly about the problem, and private time was permitted.

THE ROLE OF THE PARALLEL PLANNING COMMITTEE

When parties do not have enough trust and are concerned about the potential success of the mutual gains negotiations process, a "parallel planning committee" may be used. This committee plans the negotiations in preparation for a disaster scenario and determines what to do in the event of a strike or a lockout.

The primary objective in mutual gains negotiations is to boost the probability of generating mutual gains solutions based on the common interests. If you explore the process as we describe in this book, the probability of finding common interest solutions is high. Nevertheless, parties never know what the results of a negotiation will be.

The parties are always speculating about what might happen if they negotiate an agreement based upon interest, and they compare this expected result to what might occur through a rights or power agreement. Sometimes a party anticipates that a solution using the rights or power approach may be better than the interest-based solution. As Chapter 2 describes, the minimum standard is that the interest-based solution has to be equal to or better than what might have resulted from the rights or power approaches.

Exploring Power and Rights

As a result, it is very important for parties to know their power and rights before actually negotiating. In many cases each team of negotiators will explore its rights and power separately. In more complex negotiations, however, a separate parallel planning committee may be established to do this.

The parallel planning committee has the positive effect of not tainting the thought process of the negotiators who are attempting to reach a mutual gains agreement at the negotiating table. It ensures that the mutual gains results are truly equal to or better than what might have resulted from a rights or power approach. If parties do not resolve their dispute through the mutual gains process, the committee explores the rights and power approach.

An analogy to this process is the method by which countries engage in peace negotiations. While the negotiators discuss mutual gains in the peace talks, the military prepares for a potential war. They train soldiers, identify alternative sources of supply, and allocate funds to the war effort. All this work may be wasted energy. In the unfortunate event that it is necessary, however, the countries haven't waited until they are under attack to begin the planning process.

In exploring the rights approach, both the negotiating team and the parallel planning committee identify the precedents related to the situation and ask questions that include the following:

- What rights does each party have? What duty does each party have to the other?

- What benchmarks and precedents would be accepted by an unbiased mediator?

- What rights solution would be acceptable by a biased mediator for your side or for the other side?

- Will your solution become a "rights" precedent for other solutions?

Parallel planning committees also explore methods to enhance their power. To assess whether an interest-based solution is equal to or better than one generated by a power approach, each party has to determine what its power is in the negotiations.

In this discussion, "power" reflects what you can do unilaterally if you choose to act on your own. For example, if you are negotiating to buy a house and you are not sure whether to buy it, your decision not to purchase the house is your power. You can increase your power by having the choice of a second house to purchase. If the other party knows you are looking at a second house, your power is increased.

The seller has power by not accepting your offer. If the seller has three agents trying to buy the house at any given moment, his or her power increases because of the alternatives.

In one situation, a union's power was greater than the company's because the company had to have some way to store product in the event of a strike and could not find one. The parallel planning committee identified an alternative warehouse the company could use in the event of a strike. At the outset of negotiations, the company communicated this fact so that the union understood the extent of the power the company now had. The union walked out of the meeting but returned later. They recognized that there was a power shift and that the negotiating had to proceed under those new conditions.

The Ultimate Power—Strike or Lockout

In union-management bargaining, the ultimate power is a strike or a lockout. As an alternative solution for an unacceptable agreement, a parallel planning committee plans a strike or lockout and explores what would be done in either event. From the company perspective, plans are made to stay in business during a strike. The union, on the other hand, plans to grow the strike fund. When it comes time for an agreement to be concluded, the parallel planning committee and the negotiators discuss whether the negotiated agreement is better than the strike or lockout alternatives.

Good negotiators never take a strike or a lockout without planning. The parallel planning committee plans for a strike in the same way the negotiating team plans for an agreement. If the union strikes, it does so because striking is a better alternative than accepting the offer on the table.

The parallel planning committee attempts to enhance the potential results of rights and power because these become the minimum standard for a common-interest solution. If there is unequal power, the weaker party attempts to find ways to increase its power. Parties must be very cautious about playing the power card because once it is used, it is lost. Power is not a replenishable resource. Parties are weaker after they play their power. A party's strength lies in the other party's anticipation of his or her power.

In the 1994–95 baseball strike, both the players and the owners were caught on this issue. The players chose a deadline of August 1994, at which point they would strike. They assumed the owners would make a deal. Instead, the owners countered with a deadline—if the players didn't meet it, they would cancel the remaining season. The owners believed that the anticipation of that power would force a conclusion to the deal. Neither side had an effective planning committee determining what to do if a negotiated agreement could not be reached. Partially because the method of negotiating was ineffective, an agreement was not reached and the season was canceled.

But even if it appears that a power approach needs to be used, a fundamental negotiating principle is to never be too stubborn on a particular point. If the issue is very small—a few pennies here or there—making the deal in most cases is more important than having to resort to power. Only if the parties are negotiating on an important principle is it important to break this rule.

Every attempt should be made to prepare for the rights and the power solutions at the outset of negotiations. The parties can use these unilateral solutions if they cannot reach an overall mutual gains agreement. They try to increase their power and identify the potential results they can get from a rights solution. This becomes their minimum standard for their mutual gains agreement.

JOINT UNION-MANAGEMENT NEGOTIATION TRAINING

The concept of joint union-management training is foreign to many people. It conjures up fears that the training itself can make a difficult relationship worse. Nevertheless, nothing is more powerful than creating a learning environment between adversaries that is nonbinding and that allows people to build relationships and break down barriers.

The parties can come to the training without committing to proceed in a mutual gains negotiating manner. The process of learning together, doing negotiating exercises together, and engaging in creative brainstorming builds relationships and helps the parties realize they have more in common than they thought. When training of this kind is done effectively, the union and management representatives almost always feel that it will be of value to try negotiating in this manner.

The selection of the facilitator to assist with the training is an essential part of the planning process and can be done jointly by the union and the management. The facilitator should consider building relationships separately with the union and the company and should never be the messenger from one side to the other as a conciliator would operate. In independent discussions with union and company representatives, the facilitator gains an understanding of their needs and issues and explains how the process will proceed. At the conclusion of those individual meetings, the groups can agree to nonbinding training, which means they will proceed with the training and decide afterwards whether they want to negotiate in this manner.

Joint training is far superior to separate training in mutual gains negotiating. When training is conducted separately, each party often complains that the other party will not negotiate in the style they have learned. While the training may help the parties plan effectively, it often contributes to confusion in the way they actually negotiate because the parties have different perspectives about the process. Invariably, both sides abandon what they learned and revert back to the lowest common denominator, which is often a positional and personality-driven negotiating style.

In our experience, joint training is a key to success in mutual gains negotiating. When union and management want to engage in mutual gains negotiating and yet go through separate training, the success rate of negotiating in this manner is reduced dramatically. The opportunity to build trust in a learning environment is lost. The parties may know how to negotiate, but they do not believe the other side is willing to engage in it as they believe they want to do it. As a result, they are not as willing to proceed because they are skeptical about the other side. Joint training has tremendous potential to overcome those trust barriers.

Use Joint Training to Explore How to Overcome Barriers to Mutual Gains Negotiations

At the conclusion of joint training, the parties should answer several questions, which include:

- What are the barriers to implementing mutual gains negotiations?
- How can these barriers be overcome?
- What specific steps do we have to take so that we can engage in mutual gains negotiations?

The company and union representatives respond to the questions together and plan how to overcome the barriers. Then they determine which steps are appropriate to make the process successful.

Once the training program is completed, some analysis of the steps will be needed. Independently, the company and the union will plan their strategies for conducting surveys, identifying issues, and receiving approval to proceed with negotiations.

CONDUCT INTERNAL AND EXTERNAL SURVEYS

At the early stages of planning, the surveying and auditing process can take on many forms. For both companies and unions, the most common survey is of their key stakeholders, who identify the issues to be negotiated.

Typically, the union canvasses its membership for its demands and collects them. These demands are reviewed (vetted)—often at a convention—and then a list of demands is presented to the company before the negotiations. The list can be as long as 200 items, with several parts within each item. One nurses' union had a list of 375 demands, including fixing the stuffed toilets.

The union has a responsibility to present all the demands its membership wants to present. It clearly prefers demands that affect the collective need rather than those that reflect individual needs. However, the union has to put forward almost every demand because of its responsibility to its community. It also has the opportunity to change the way demands are collected and the precise content of their surveys.

In mutual gains negotiations, unions may still collect demands, but those demands are used only when the negotiating parties begin to explore creative solutions. In addition to asking its membership for their demands, unions ask for the problems or opportunities they see. They bring the problems to the negotiating table at the outset of negotiations. The demands are saved for later in the negotiations as potential solutions to those problems are considered.

Until a few years ago, companies rarely put proposals to the union on the negotiating table. In most cases, they attempted to achieve a status quo result from negotiations. Their preparation focused on anticipating the union's demands. They typically ask the following:

- What are the problems, opportunities, and needs for the future of my counterpart?

- What issues would be of greatest importance to my counterpart?

- What would be strike or lockout issues?

- What would be the costing associated with my counterpart's proposal?
- What do I believe are the important issues, and what are the issues of less importance?

After the recession of the early 1990s, management has begun to analyze the frustrations in different parts of their enterprises. They also have been placing demands on the negotiating table. Their method has been similar to that of unions. They "propose" specific solutions and want the union to accept them. In mutual gains negotiating, the company puts forth its problems, not its solutions. The expectation is that through joint problem solving, the company and the union will develop solutions that are in the mutual interest.

Companies also analyze the terms of other contracts in similar businesses, especially ones in which the union with whom they are negotiating has membership. With this analysis they can foresee some of the issues that might be a precedent for their organization. This information will also become useful in generating a mandate.

Companies and unions conduct other surveys and audits. These include the following:

1. Negotiating planners often conduct quantitative and qualitative analyses on the previous negotiations to determine what may be the issues for the current negotiation.

2. Some organizations engage in conflict audits. These audits explore the losses and potential losses due to conflict and the kinds of conflicts that produce these losses. Next, the organizations determine who might benefit by reducing the conflict. That leads to strategy development to prevent and/or reduce the losses identified. The strategy can be developed jointly between the company and the union to begin creating a climate of trust and collaboration.

3. An external resource may conduct an attitudinal audit. This audit assesses how ready all parties are to engage in mutual gains negotiations and to determine what needs to be done to enhance that readiness. Usually, the agreement to do this audit is part of the action plans completed during joint training in mutual gains negotiations.

In enlightened companies, union and management are willing to share the information they learn at this point. This sets the stage for understanding what issues will be brought to negotiations rather than being surprised.

In traditional bargaining, demands and proposals are identified instead of problems. The assumption is that you negotiate solutions rather than try to identify problems and reach a common-interest solution. In mutual gains, the parties identify problems, opportunities, and needs for the future to discuss with counterparts during negotiations.

PRESENT ISSUES FOR APPROVAL TO NEGOTIATE

In most negotiations, the negotiators need approval or agreement to present issues, problems, or opportunities at a negotiating table. Unions often have to bring their issues and proposals to the membership for approval. Sometimes the national union is involved in agreeing with the direction that the local union negotiators will take.

From a company perspective, senior management plays a major role in determining what issues will and will not be negotiated. Nothing captures the imagination of senior management like the potential of a strike or a lockout. One senior executive said he takes a great deal of interest in collective bargaining because it is the only process that can totally shut the company down. It is also the only planning process that results in a three-year plan and a contract requiring the company to operate in accordance with that plan. Most companies have trouble planning for more than one quarter of a year.

In mutual gains negotiating, it is sometimes difficult to persuade senior managers to trust negotiators to produce the deal. Senior managers may be more comfortable dealing with demands and counterdemands than experimenting with joint resolution of problems. Their lack of trust is a potential barrier to successful mutual gains negotiating. But if they are willing to engage in training on mutual gains negotiating, they will understand the process and the kinds of issues and problems that will be brought to them. The same kind of training should occur for both the company and the union senior leadership.

The Mandate for Negotiations

Mandate is a term that is most commonly used by management. The term has a different meaning in traditional bargaining and mutual gains negotiating. The differences are:

- In traditional bargaining, *mandate* means the specific results senior leadership wants the negotiators to accomplish.

- In mutual gains negotiations, *mandate* means the line below which you resort to power. In other words, it's your bottom line.

Essentially, negotiating parties need to know what their mandates are. In traditional bargaining, senior executives tell the negotiators what they want to get, sometimes in great detail— line by line, problem by problem. They demand a specific solution, and the negotiators have to find a way to navigate to that solution. In the mutual gains approach, where a mandate is the point beyond which you resort to power, you can attempt to negotiate wise and simple solutions as long as you do not have to resort to power. The negotiators are given a total package mandate, and they have the mandate to make strong recommendations. The latitude of the negotiators increases significantly and is the preferred way to proceed with this process.

In mutual gains negotiating, you must get a mandate that focuses on that bottom line. It is essential to effective management by the senior group who ultimately have to support the decisions of the negotiators.

Mandate Presentations to the Company

A company's mandate is usually generated through sophisticated technology and analysis. In the collective labor negotiations process, the mandate presentation to the company's senior leadership includes:

1. A section that describes all the matters related to **monetary issues,** including wages, time off, compensation and benefits, and duration of the agreement.

2. A clear definition of the **major issues** that are potential strike/lockout issues for both sides. The mandate usually includes a minimum of three company issues and three union issues. Examples describing the issues and their implications need to be clearly defined so that the mandate presentation is fully understood.

3. A detailed chart comparing the **compensation package** for the company as it compares to its major competitors. To make the comparison, characteristics of the workforce can be compared to a major competitor's contract. The compensation chart defines what a person in your company would be paid on an hourly or annual basis if your competitor's contract was used in your company. The list includes:

    *   All compensation issues—compensation per hour, cost of living allowance (if any), vacation pay, holiday pay, taxes, social assistance.
    *   All benefits, including coverage for medical, disabilities, extended health, maternity allowance, dental, and so on.
    *   The company pension plan.

Next, total dollar values for the company and the comparison companies are generated. From that, the company's bottom-line target can be determined. This information is useful to establish parameters so the negotiators will know what they can negotiate when they consider the financial package.

4. The mandate concludes with **the best deal the company can offer** the union. If the union is preparing a mandate, it will be the minimum it is willing to take based on its rights and power analysis from the comparisons with other contracts.

To succeed at developing a meaningful mandate, internal negotiations have to take place. In their landmark book *A Behavioral Theory of Labor Negotiations,* Walton and McKersie state that at least three negotiations occur at any one time in collective bargaining.[12] The obvious negotiation is the one between the union and the company. Perhaps the more difficult negotiations occur between the union and its membership, or its national entity, and between the company negotiators and senior management.

Essential to effective mutual gains negotiating is the ability of the union and company to resolve the differences between the central players within their own constituencies. Every attempt should be made to settle these differences before the actual negotiations begin.

In one situation, the employer and the union were negotiating for modifications to the job evaluation system. They agreed to a pilot process to develop an interim language that would last for a specific period of time. The agreement authorized the union to engage in pilot studies, but past experience indicated that the union's membership would approve of the union pilot studies only if all employees ratified the idea. Some of the managers were also concerned that the negotiators agreed to a pilot study when they were not fully consulted. They felt they were "painted into a corner" and therefore had no choice but to agree.

In this situation, although management and the union agreed to proceed with the pilot study, their relationship was the only strength in their process. They were concerned about how they were going to negotiate with their own constituencies to ensure agreement with their direction. They were also worried that there might be significant dissatisfaction with the changes they were suggesting.

Some strategies to smooth the resolution of internal differences include:

- Involving some senior leaders in the mutual gains training process.

- Including some senior leaders on the negotiating team.

- Setting up a formal communication network or "gate" review process (see Chapter 9) to help senior leaders know what is being negotiated.

- Ensuring that the negotiators are respected by the leaders who are not at the table so those leaders will value the solutions that are generated.

The Value of Mutual Gains Negotiations for Internal Negotiations with Constituencies

Sometimes one party wants to proceed with mutual gains negotiations and the other wants to negotiate in the traditional adversarial manner. In one case the union rejected mutual gains negotiations, claiming it was really a management trick. They argued that they would be at a disadvantage because of management's strong problem-solving skills, while the union representatives had done very well using the old approach.

When only one party wants to play, the basic engineering principle applies: "An object moves as fast as its slowest part." The process often regresses to the lowest common denominator. The union that rejected mutual gains negotiating in the above case might have to spend more time building trust. Parties might also have to begin operating in a mutual gains manner on a day-to-day basis before they trust each other enough to apply this approach.

The Benefits of Mutual Gains Negotiating during the Planning Phase

Nevertheless, mutual gains negotiating in the planning phase is very important to the negotiators even if one of the parties does not want to negotiate that way. The following are some of the benefits:

- Even if the negotiations are adversarial, mutual gains negotiating planning enhances the quality of the demands because they will likely be in the common interest rather than in the interest of one party alone.

- Mutual gains negotiating helps resolve disputes among a team of negotiators within one party, including differences of direction they want to propose, both to their own constituencies and to their counterparts.

- Mutual gains negotiating helps the parties negotiate with internal leadership. The internal negotiations include developing the mandate to negotiate and the power to make decisions or present strong recommendations during negotiations.

SIMULATING THE NEGOTIATIONS DURING PLANNING

When the parties trust the process and each other, the planning time may represent about 25 percent of the negotiations. When trust is low, the planning time increases to as much as 50 percent of the negotiations process. The planning time includes a variety of activities, but a major part of the planning phase is the simulation of the entire negotiations, which is described in this section.

Preparing Problem Resolution When Trust Is High

The typical planning process for parties when their trust in the process and each other is high is as follows:

- Identify your problems and anticipate the problems of your counterparts.
- Explore the facts and clarify your own interests on each problem.
- Proceed to the actual negotiations with a mandate to negotiate the best possible agreement within certain dollar parameters.

Preparing Problem Resolution When Trust Is Low

When the parties' trust is low, the largest part of the planning time is devoted to a simulation of the negotiations using mutual gains negotiations. The process is as follows:

- Identify your problems and anticipate the problems of your counterparts.
- Clarify facts.
- Speculate about what the common interests are.
- Engage in creative brainstorming.
- Anticipate the potential solutions for each problem.
- Identify your preferred solution.

The last three steps require a large amount of time. Most excellent debaters know that the best way to master an issue is to be able to debate your counterpart's position effectively. Negotiations are no different. You need to speculate about how you would negotiate the situation from your counterpart's viewpoint. The benefit of this exercise is to maximize the quality of thought during negotiations. As a result, nothing is a surprise to these negotiators. They are ready to consider all interests from the perspective of their counterparts as well as their internal constituencies. They even understand their counterparts' problems (or the ones they assume they will have). They develop this understanding just as they would in any good debate. In negotiations, the parties use the same analysis process for their problems and their counterparts' problems.

Some may argue that this analysis will eliminate the spontaneity of the actual negotiations, but in high-risk, low-trust situations, spontaneity is not of high value. However, parties should be open to their counterparts' interests and recognize other creative solutions they did not consider. When trust is low and there is concern about how negotiations will proceed, an extensive planning process reduces risk.

APPLYING MUTUAL GAINS TOGETHER DURING THE PLANNING PHASE

Union and management negotiators sometimes begin collaborating before contract negotiations. This sometimes occurs after joint training. In those sessions they may select pilot areas in which they can experiment in mutual gains negotiating before applying it to collective bargaining. Using this approach on a problem in an area such as health and safety enables the parties to learn and experiment together and build a model that works for them without the pressure of timelines. They then can use that model when they engage in actual collective bargaining.

After the parties complete their collaboration on the pilot problems, they can review what worked and what did not work. This review is done before contract negotiations begin to determine how the process needs to be modified for negotiations. The following are some actions they may take in the preliminary review process:

- Identify the parties' ability to resolve problems before beginning mutual gains negotiations.
- Identify the measures by which this mutual gains negotiations process should be assessed.

- Determine whether what was achieved in the pilot case study has a positive return on investment in terms of time, cost, and relationships.

- Assess each component of the mutual gains negotiations process to determine which can be modified to enhance the ability of the parties to solve problems jointly.

- Identify the activities that should "start," those that should "stop," and those that should "continue" in order to use the mutual gains negotiations process in collective bargaining.

After the parties complete that review, they follow the process as they have modified it. Frequently, the review generates recommendations that will help the parties in the negotiations process. Two recommendations that may result from the review are (1) a method of speeding up the negotiations and (2) a way to ensure that the parties do not depart from the mutual gains negotiations method when they address more contentious issues.

After the pilot study, it is also useful for the parties to discuss how to orient their constituencies to this method of negotiation. When parties communicate a promise of success without a real-life example, the constituencies' responses are often cynical and skeptical. It is a far better communication strategy to use a real pilot success to demonstrate that mutual gains problem solving can really work.

COMPLETING THE PLANNING PHASE

When planning is done effectively, negotiators feel ready for almost any eventuality. They are confident that they did everything they could to generate mutual gains solutions that benefit all parties. They are also optimistic that if the mutual gains process is unsuccessful, they have a fallback plan that is well thought out.

They enter into contract negotiations with the core capabilities to achieve a mutual gains agreement. These include:

- **The knowledge and understanding of the negotiation problems.** Parties feel confident in the legitimacy of their problems and interests.

- **Effective relationships built internally.** The parties have created efficient communications and good working relationships among their own team members. They are committed to each other and have self-help options if negotiations become difficult.

- **The ability to keep a constant eye on two or three key principles.** The parties are ready for any direct or indirect challenges to them on core principles.

- **The problem-solving skills to do mutual gains negotiations internally as well as with their counterparts.** Joint training and planning help the negotiators have the confidence that they can succeed with mutual gains negotiations. If they resolve a joint pilot problem together, they have a real-life experience they can refer to to prove it can be done.

Although the prenegotiation planning is complete, the planning continues throughout the negotiations. The negotiators need time to meet and review the progress of the negotiations, compare the actual progress with their expectations, and modify their planned direction. They need to be responsive and flexible to the surprises that invariably occur in collective bargaining.

Detailed planning helps the negotiators focus on problem resolution rather than personalities. As a result of this planning, they will be able to negotiate with full awareness of what they are doing and reach an agreement that achieves mutual gains for all parties.

SUMMARY

- The five phases are of mutual gains negotiating are:
  - Phase 1—Planning.

- – Phase 2—Getting Started with Face-to-Face Negotiations.
  - – Phase 3—Mutual Gains Problem Solving.
  - – Phase 4—Reaching Agreement.
  - – Phase 5—Living by the Agreement.
- • In the planning process, several crucial aspects are important. These are:
  - – Identifying the negotiating team members.
  - – Mutual commitments within a negotiating team.
  - – The role of the "back room" in negotiations.
  - – The role of a "parallel planning committee."
  - – Joint union-management negotiation training.
  - – Conducting internal and external surveys.
  - – Presenting issues for approval to negotiate.
  - – Simulating the negotiations process during planning.
  - – Completing the planning phase.
- • The negotiating team you select sends an important message to your counterparts. The negotiating team should have some professional negotiators, but the majority should be the managers or employees within the union or the company.
- • Perhaps the most important person on a negotiating team is the chief spokesperson.
- • In the planning process, the negotiating team makes commitments about how the members will work together during the negotiations.
- • The "back room" is a useful idea in any kind of negotiation. Essentially, a planning room is set up prior to negotiations that continues to exist for the duration of the bargaining process.
- • The back room can have many valuable functions. Since the negotiating parties may interpret the function of the back room incorrectly, it is important at the outset to

explain why the back room exists and how it adds value to the negotiation process.

- In negotiations in which a high level of trust has been established, the company and union representatives can perform many of the back-room functions jointly.

- When parties do not have enough trust and are concerned about the potential success of the mutual gains negotiations process, a "parallel planning committee" may be used. This committee plans the negotiations in preparation for a disaster and determines what to do in the event of a strike or a lockout.

- In union-management bargaining, the ultimate power is a strike or a lockout. As an alternative solution for an unacceptable agreement, a parallel planning committee plans a strike or lockout and explores what would be done in either event.

- The concept of joint union-management training is foreign to many people. It conjures up fears that the training itself can make a difficult relationship worse. Nevertheless, nothing is more powerful than creating a learning environment between adversaries that is "nonbinding" to allow people to build relationships and break down barriers.

- The selection of the facilitator to assist with the training is an essential part of the planning process and can be done jointly by the union and the management.

- Most excellent debaters know that the best way to master an issue is to be able to debate your counterpart's position effectively. Negotiations are no different. You need to speculate about how you would negotiate from your counterpart's viewpoint.

- At the early stages of planning for contract negotiations, the surveying and auditing process can take on many forms.

- Typically, the union canvasses its membership for its demands and collects them. These demands are reviewed (vetted)—often at a convention—and then a list of demands is presented to the company prior to the negotiations. In the mutual gains negotiations process, unions may still collect demands, but those demands are used only when the negotiating parties begin to discover creative solutions.

- Companies have also been placing demands on the negotiating table. They "propose" specific solutions and want the union to accept them. In mutual gains negotiating, the company puts forth its problems, not its solutions. The expectation is that through joint problem solving, the company and the union will develop solutions that are in the mutual interest.

- Unions often have to bring their issues and proposals to the membership for approval. Sometimes the national union is involved in agreeing with the direction that the local union negotiators will take. From a company perspective, senior management plays a major role in determining what issues will and will not be negotiated.

- *Mandate* is a term that is most commonly used by management.

  - In traditional bargaining, *mandate* means the results the senior leadership wants the negotiators to accomplish.

  - In mutual gains negotiations, *mandate* means the line below which you resort to power. In other words, it's your bottom line.

- Mutual gains negotiating enhances the quality of the demands, helps resolve disputes among parties, and helps parties negotiate with internal leadership.

- When trust is low and there is concern about how negotiations will proceed, an extensive planning process reduces risk.

CHAPTER 5

Getting Started with Face-to-Face Negotiations

Once the parties set the stage for the negotiations through joint training and planning, they are ready to move to Phase 2. In mutual gains negotiations, getting started with face-to-face negotiations is not a dramatic event. The tension is reduced because they have engaged in discussion from the time of training 9 to 12 months before negotiations, throughout the survey process, and even while identifying needs for the future.

You can almost predict the success of the mutual gains approach by the extent to which people politicize the opening of negotiations. If an elaborate show is presented, it is more likely that the trust is low between the parties and that the mutual gains process will be more difficult. This chapter describes the second phase of mutual gains negotiations in detail and explores the issue of labeling the process. The following are the steps of the getting-started phase of the mutual gains process:

- Make opening statements.
- Confirm the use of the mutual gains negotiations process.
- Develop negotiating principles among the parties.

- Develop the full list of problems to be negotiated.
- Set the timelines and locations for the negotiations.
- Consider external facilitation for the first mutual gains negotiations.

MAKE OPENING STATEMENTS

The first weeks of mutual gains negotiations are markedly different from adversarial negotiations, which begin with what is known as the "photo shoot." In adversarial negotiations, the lead players make an appearance, and the photographers are there to document the opening. In attendance may be the president of the company and other senior executives, the national union president and other senior leaders of the union, and the negotiators. The parties give official statements and often serve the demands. Usually, each side engages in rhetoric about the ills the other side has foisted upon them over the years and how they hope this time the other side will come to their senses.

The mutual gains negotiations process is very different. If political positioning of the company and union leadership is necessary, there may be some fanfare. However, building a climate of mutual respect and joint problem solving is the focus. Both sides present brief opening statements, explain why they want to engage in mutual gains negotiations, and communicate their hope for success. These statements often have these characteristics:

- **They set the tone for mutual gains negotiations.** The statements often begin in a conciliatory way. Each side recognizes that the other deserves respect. They acknowledge that they are "in the same boat" and will have to get out of this difficult situation with a new style of negotiations.

- **They emphasize the importance of not having status differences.** All negotiators are equal problem solvers and share responsibility to resolve the problems facing each party.

- **They express the hope for the negotiations.** Parties should clearly state central facts that are relevant to the entire negotiations. For example, parties sometimes review market changes, financial successes or problems of the past years, and successes or problems in union-management relations. However, they should avoid references to power in the opening statements.

After making opening statements, the parties identify the principles on which they will negotiate. These principles do not include logistics such as the time for breaks or the length of the meetings. Rather, they are the guiding negotiating principles that will help make the negotiations proceed effectively. Parties usually include the principle of resolving problems through the mutual gains process. The next section describes what the mutual gains process entails. This description is followed by a detailed exploration of what is often included in the complete list of negotiating principles.

CONFIRM USING THE MUTUAL GAINS PROBLEM-SOLVING PROCESS

Negotiations proceed more smoothly if the negotiators agree to follow a model like the one presented here. This model has been used in numerous negotiations and was developed by assessing how mutual gains negotiators actually manage the process. Many experts suggest that mutual gains negotiating is an art form, but to teach mutual gains negotiating and communicate how it is done, it is necessary to systematically identify the components of the process and develop a model.

The model is in a simple, linear format so that negotiators can understand and apply it to their situations. After negotiators have gained experience in applying the model, they will be more confident of their flexibility and will vary from the design as necessary.

Figure 5–1 is the model used to help negotiators work through the mutual gains problem-solving process. Each of these

FIGURE 5-1

Mutual Gains Problem-Solving Model

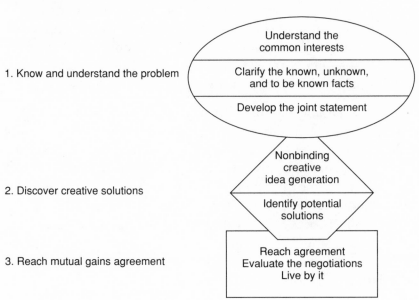

1. Know and understand the problem

2. Discover creative solutions

3. Reach mutual gains agreement

steps is discussed in detail in subsequent chapters. The following is a brief look at each of the steps in the model.

Know and Understand the Problem

The circular "bubble" image in Figure 5–1 depicts the steps that parties must explore before entertaining solutions. The parties need to understand the interests common to both parties and those unique to each. Next, they must fully disclose the known, the unknown, and the knowable, verifiable facts. They make this disclosure so that each party can use the same information to make a decision. Then, the parties should identify the stakeholders and agree on the problem that requires resolution. Typically, 25 percent of the time on any problem is spent on knowing and understanding it before any solutions are entertained.

Identifying the common interests, the facts, and the joint problem statement provides the opportunity to stimulate the creative solutions necessary to make the negotiation as successful as possible.

Discover Creative Solutions

The "diamond" in Figure 5–1 illustrates the expansion required in divergent thought, which eventually is closed when reaching solutions. To increase the possibility that the mutual gains solutions are wise and simple, parties need to expand their minds and brainstorm as many ideas as possible. This will ensure that the parties consider all possible alternatives about the problem.

To achieve a result that is equal to or better than what might have emerged in traditional bargaining, the parties must then converge the ideas and assess the solutions very carefully. They must also consider who the stakeholders are and who the winners and losers will be. The parties need to identify any unintentional losers and explore methods to reduce the negative effects of that loss to those stakeholders.

The delay that might occur as a result of this analysis is not excessive. The quality mutual gains solution that is good enough today will be good enough tomorrow as well. Reflection time is encouraged to make sure that parties generate quality conclusions.

Reach Mutual Gains Agreements

The box in Figure 5–1 represents a solution that is clean, simple, and wise. The purpose of the mutual gains process is to reach agreements that all parties can support. Attention is given to ongoing dialogue and continuous negotiations to ensure that the agreement can be put into operation.

Is the Model Always Followed?

Parties often step through the negotiation process as shown in the model and then backtrack several times. Backtracking is necessary to do the following:

- Refine what the joint problem might be.
- Add relevant facts.

- Reflect on additional interests.
- Consider new ideas that will contribute to the wisest, simplest solution to the problem and enhance the quality of the relationships.

Additionally, while following the process is a key success factor, it should never be a burden. It should add value to the problem resolution and not become a barrier to reaching agreement. For example, some problems have obvious solutions to which all parties can agree immediately. It would be a waste of time and emotional energy to use the process. Instead, the parties should agree to the solution and move on to the next problem.

Alternatively, it may be useful with some problems to know up front what each side wants in order to understand the magnitude of the differences. Sometimes this can help the parties focus their discussion of interests and facts. Following the process, though, still remains a key success factor because it is the foundation to which the parties return regularly as they deviate to reach agreements.

The experienced mutual gains negotiator knows when to alter the process and how to return gracefully. Sometimes parties use a skilled facilitator to guide the process. Just as a tour guide knows the roads on which to travel, the skilled facilitator navigates the journey to reach an agreement. Novice negotiators would be wise to stay much closer to the mutual gains process, for they may not know how to return to the path once they deviate and become lost.

The Extent to Which Mutual Gains Problem Solving Can Be Applied

The mutual gains bargaining process can be used when the issues lend themselves to collaborative problem solving. Sometimes the parties may not have enough trust to discuss certain issues openly, so mutual gains negotiating is used only partially for issues.

Negotiators need to accept this variability so that they do not feel as if they are failing when mutual gains negotiating does not work completely.

For example, negotiators might be willing to clarify the problem and generate common interests using mutual gains negotiating and then decide to present their demands based upon this information. The demands will be closer together than had the negotiators not reached that understanding of the problem and the parties' interests. The information sharing that took place in mutual gains negotiating will enhance subsequent traditional negotiations.

DEVELOP NEGOTIATING PRINCIPLES AMONG THE PARTIES

Before exploring the problem, parties need to determine the negotiating principles. The principles are useful to ensure that the parties will follow the new style of negotiating. They function as a common set of ground rules. With these principles and a common understanding of what they want to accomplish, the parties can negotiate in good faith.

Perhaps the best way to have quality negotiating principles is for the parties to engage in joint training. As a result of this training, a common mind-set emerges that increases the willingness of the parties to consider a more collaborative method of negotiations and dispute resolution. At the conclusion of training, it is more likely that the groups will explore negotiating principles that are consistent with the joint problem-solving approach recommended here.

The first mutual gains agreement the parties encounter is the agreement to a common set of negotiating principles. This preliminary agreement should be relatively easy and a good beginning to the process. When it becomes difficult, it may be a sign of laborious negotiations to come.

The groups should address two questions: What would be a terrific negotiation process for all parties? What would be a terrible negotiation process for all parties? We emphasize that this is the negotiation principle about the *process*, not the *outcome*.

It will also be valuable to identify what the specific players' roles will be in the negotiations with particular emphasis on the spokespeople and the facilitators. Spokespeople have a less dominant role in the mutual gains approach because everyone has an opportunity to talk. Facilitators increase their importance because everybody has opportunities to facilitate at different times. The same two questions can be asked about the role of the facilitators: What would be terrific facilitation? What would be terrible facilitation?

The groups generate the responses that help them identify how they might proceed with negotiations. In effect, this represents the first mini-negotiation between the parties. Because it is so early in the process, it is often their first success in reaching a mutual gains solution on how they want to negotiate.

Parties vary in the principles they consider and use in negotiations. The extent of the detail varies depending on the amount of trust between the parties. Some of the principles include:

- **Honesty.** The negotiators are expected to mean what they say and say what they mean. In addition, they agree to live up to what they say they will do. This is consistent with the second level of trust described in Chapter 3.

- **Follow the mutual gains problem-solving process.** Often people allow their emotions to moderate the mutual gains process, making it less probable they will reach effective solutions. If they follow the process and the steps, they can remain focused and reach an effective mutual gains solution. This principle was identified as a key success factor in Chapter 1.

- **Deal with the problems and not the personalities.** Personalities are an essential part of any dispute resolution. The emotion that emerges from a focus on personalities always supersedes the intellectual process. Parties will be more effective in this process if they focus on problems rather than personalities.

- **Decision by consensus.** The Saturn Autoworkers and Saturn GM management use an effective approach toward consensus. Their principle is that if all the parties feel they can agree to at least 70 percent of a decision (i.e., they can live with it), they will be committed 100 percent to the decision. They refer to this approach as "70 Percent Agreement and 100 Percent Commitment."

- **Negotiators have the authority to make a decision or a strong recommendation.** For constructive discussions to occur and resolution to be achieved, negotiate with those who have a full understanding of the problems and the authority to make decisions. Negotiators should understand the authority of the chief spokespeople so that the groups will know what level of decision they can reach. If a negotiator knows the limits of the spokesperson's authority, he or she can understand why delays occur later in the negotiations.

- **Joint planning of confidentiality and communications.** The parties should decide jointly what will be confidential and what will be communicated. The most conservative approach is that the negotiations are totally confidential unless otherwise specified. Information is often communicated independently and rarely as a joint union-management release. An example of such an agreement appears at the end of Chapter 7.

The negotiating parties also agree to the kind of communication devices they will use and what will be the content of the communication. For example, some negotiators feel that the only way they can create change is to communicate through the media. When this occurs, however, parties lose trust. The recommended standard response to media inquiries should be, "We are making progress."

In addition, the parties typically agree that they will not write any independent reports about the content of the mutual gains negotiations even if the negotiations do not resolve effectively. With this kind of confidentiality and communications agreement, the negotiating parties can be more open with each other throughout the negotiations process.

Example of Negotiating Principles in Mutual Gains Negotiations

In one negotiation, the parties developed a simple list of negotiation principles. They kept the handwritten list on the wall throughout a three-month negotiation process. Their principles were:

- Honesty.
- Trust.
- No hidden agendas.
- Nonbinding brainstorming.
- Equal partner through discussions.
- Examine all related information.
- No reprisals as a result of discussions.
- No deal is done until the entire deal is done.
- All discussions are confidential unless agreed to otherwise.
- Only records are the agreed-upon flip chart notes.
- Joint planning of communications.

In another situation, the negotiators developed their negotiating principles into a list of dos and don'ts. This list is what they developed:

DO	DON'T
Focus on problems, not personalities	Trap yourself into positional bargaining
Focus on common ground and the vision of the preferred future	Attack and irritate people or be cynical about the process
Search for opportunities to build and explore new ideas	Oversell your ideas too forcefully
Work to reduce tension and create synergy	Become inflexible and limit your exploration
Build a network of constructive progress	Close your mind
Consider all perspectives, especially others'	Consider only your own perspective
Challenge constructively	Use pressure tactics

DEVELOP THE FULL LIST OF PROBLEMS TO BE NEGOTIATED

The most important part of the opening session is for parties to identify jointly the problems that will form the agenda for the negotiations. This discussion can take as few as three days and, in some negotiations, as many as the first two weeks of negotiations.

In some cases, because of legislation requirements, one of the parties may have written the problems and opportunities and given them in advance to the other party. In one of the more adversarial negotiation situations, a union actually mailed its demands to the company and did not even want to see them face-to-face.

In the mutual gains approach, the union and the company review all the problems and opportunities at an initial meeting that usually takes one week. Both parties present the problems they are bringing to the negotiation. The problems may have come from internal and/or external surveys and from their own reflections on the challenges facing their constituencies at that time.

The parties review and discuss the list of problems to ensure that each understands the facts and interests associated with the problems. This takes place even if there is no agreement about whether the problems should be negotiated items. The parties then cluster the long list of problems into several groups. Each problem is entered into a group regardless of whether the union or management presented it. A full agenda emerges from this process that enables both parties to know the following:

- The timelines for the negotiations.

- When certain experts will be needed.

- The best location for negotiating specific problems.

The order of the problems on the agenda is an important issue to consider. The best way for parties to build trust in each other is to address the problems in the common interest first.

Next, the parties address issues that will require some separate interests to be reflected in the solution of the problem. These are more complicated issues to which solutions are possible but will require more give-and-take for the parties to be comfortable with their agreement.

The issues in the third group are those whose solution seems elusive. These issues appear to be zero-sum problems such as negotiating the monetary package. The company wants to give less, the union wants more, and only a fixed amount of money seems to be available. In many situations, however, parties can apply mutual gains problem solving to these kinds of issues because of the trust they have built by resolving earlier problems.

In one negotiation, the union representative felt job security was a core issue because it was a foundation problem and should be dealt with early in the process. The union assumed that job security might not be a common interest with management and, therefore, the parties might deal with it too late in the process. After careful consideration, the union and the company agreed to resolve several problems that appeared to be in the common interest. They then proceeded to work on foundation problems— job security being one of them.

No magic formula exists for the order in which problems should be addressed. However, parties are advised to explore easier problems before entertaining and resolving the more difficult and contentious ones so that they can build a reservoir of trust and success.

After the parties identify the problems and set the agenda, they often recognize that they need a generic set of facts for the negotiations to proceed effectively. The parties may plan to present these facts (usually by the company and sometimes by the union) at the first meeting after the "getting-started" session. The generic facts will be useful throughout the negotiations as the parties explore the interests, facts, and joint problem statements for a wide range of issues.

THE EASE AND THE DIFFICULTY OF APPLYING MUTUAL GAINS NEGOTIATIONS

Some problems lend themselves to mutual gains negotiations more readily than others. The ease with which parties are willing to use this process varies depending on the nature of the problem. The following are three types of problems:

1. **The easiest kind of problem to deal with.** When both parties have the same problem, the problem will be the easiest to deal with. Here are some examples:

   - All parties agree they have a problem with the job evaluation system.

   - Everyone believes that the grievance process is ineffective.

   - All parties see that there is a significant health and safety issue in one environment.

In situations like this, the mutual gains negotiations process is easy to apply because everybody sees the problem as a joint problem. A union negotiator commented after mutual gains negotiations that "there is no excuse for not using mutual gains negotiations when there is a mutual problem." When parties have a joint problem and use positional bargaining tactics, both the employer and the union have lost an opportunity.

2. **The more difficult area in which to apply mutual gains negotiations.** One party presents problems that the other party would prefer not to address. But when it is evident that the reluctant party is going to experience some pain by not addressing the problem, it is more probable that mutual gains negotiations will be applied. The following are some examples:

   • Often employers would prefer not to address the monetary package and give more money to the union. If the two parties do not negotiate a satisfactory monetary package, however, the union may stop work through a strike or slowdowns. The pain associated with work stoppage will create a sense of urgency about the need to listen to the union's interests and to negotiate an agreement.

   • When a company wants to restructure work so that employees are multiskilled, the union may not want to consider this possibility. However, the company can unilaterally implement changes if it is part of its management rights. To avoid the pain of a unilateral decision by the company, the union may engage in mutual gains negotiations on this issue.

3. **The most difficult kind of problems in which to apply mutual gains negotiations.** In every negotiation parties recognize they do not have to discuss some problems because they will experience no pain as a

result. In those cases, parties have often not applied mutual gains negotiations. The party that is not interested in discussing the problem may simply say no.

However, if uninterested parties want to build trust and explore the goodwill in the relationship, they are wise to bring the assumptions behind a request to the surface. By discussing the interests, they may identify a way to meet the real need through a response that is less distasteful to themselves. This kind of response would be at the discretion of the uninterested party. Clearly, the more the parties have enhanced their relationship, the greater the willingness for each party to listen to the other's needs on these kinds of problems.

For example, the union may request to have day care facilities or provisions to deal with child care as part of the collective agreement. The employer knows that the union will not strike on this issue or even take a work action. Sometimes, even when mutual gains negotiations are proceeding, the employer simply says no and the discussion stops at that point. If the relationship is strong enough, the employer at least engages in some dialogue with the union to understand the true underlying needs and to explore alternative mechanisms to help employees deal with the problem.

SET THE TIMELINES AND LOCATIONS FOR THE NEGOTIATIONS

After the parties have set the agenda, they can work out the specific logistics (for example, the location). While having the negotiations in one hotel is often the most convenient method, the negotiations can also be in more than one place. Travel and availability of resources for particular problems on the agenda are factors to consider.

The amount of time spent in actual negotiations is another logistic to work out. The parties need to determine what is right for them. No answer is right or wrong. Mutual gains negotiators have different preferences about the amount of time they want to negotiate in one meeting period. For example, some may want to negotiate two weeks in a row for every one week off. They can use the week off to plan meetings and catch up with other activities apart from negotiations. Others may prefer one week of negotiations and one week off. Still others may want to negotiate four days a week and have the fifth day for planning.

CONSIDER EXTERNAL FACILITATION FOR THE FIRST MUTUAL GAINS NEGOTIATIONS

Old habits die slowly. Even with the best of intentions, parties may regress to the old ways of negotiating. Many first-time mutual gains negotiators have found it useful to have external facilitation for their first attempt at this new process.

The facilitator's role is to ensure that the negotiations progress effectively. The following are characteristic of effective facilitators:

- **Fair, independent, neutral, trustworthy, and there to help both sides.** Facilitators must reflect the interests of all parties, regardless of their personal opinions on an issue. Facilitators who take sides fall out of trust and often cannot continue in that role.

  If union management negotiators act as facilitators, they also must be impartial and not show bias when they facilitate. For example, a facilitator may use the power of the Magic Marker™ to write on flip charts only what he or she believes in or may begin to dominate discussion. If bias occurs, any other person can call "switch" and have the facilitator replaced by another person without having to explain the reason.

- **Keep the parties talking in a constructive way.** Facilitators help the parties recognize they are working toward a common goal. In the end, the parties will have to find solutions to the problem.

- **Have the sensitivity to call a time-out if the parties become aggressive.** By managing the climate, facilitators ensure that people do not say things that bring them to a walkout. Controlling "the pressure in the kettle to let some steam out" is always a judgment call.

- **Keep control if others lose their temper.** Facilitators try to avoid people making statements they will regret. To relieve the stress, they may say something such as, "Why don't we cool down? It's tough on everybody." In one case the facilitator said, "The whole thing will blow up if you keep this up." By calling the aggressiveness to everyone's attention, the facilitator encouraged people to change their behavior. Facilitators may even ask if something they do not know about is contributing to the hostility.

- **Never become the go-between.** Facilitators should listen to each side but should not be the messenger from one party to the other. They always listen to people, but they should encourage parties to communicate directly with their counterparts rather than going through the facilitator. One facilitator said to a party, "You might have convinced me, but what good does that do? You have to convince them. I am not the messenger."

The Facilitator as a Provocateur

Should facilitators know as much as possible about their cases, or should they operate without any knowledge of the matters to be negotiated? This is a controversial subject. The argument is based on the issue of bias and the ability of an individual to control those biases.

The assumption is that if you know nothing, you have no potential to be biased. Therefore, some believe that the preference would be to know nothing. The alternative strategy is to know everything; however, the risk is that the facilitator will generate a bias as the result of that knowledge.

My preference is to know everything and deal with the personal limitation of bias. It is essential for the facilitator to know as much as possible about the situation through interviews and discussions without having bias and without becoming the messenger.

The facilitator needs to be thoroughly knowledgeable about the situation in order to be a provocateur, asking the tough questions and ensuring the intellectual integrity of the process. The decision of what to do remains with the parties who are actually engaged in the negotiations. The facilitator does not give solutions to the problem. He or she facilitates the discussion, which results in an answer.

The Facilitator Can Be the Problem

There are enough complications in any negotiations; the parties do not need the facilitator to be an additional burden. A very direct discussion needs to take place if the facilitator stops adding value to the negotiations. If the problems are not resolved, replace the facilitator or divide the facilitation responsibilities among the negotiating parties.

These are some of the ways facilitators can be the problem:

- *They think they know the answers better than the negotiating parties do.* Tell the facilitator: "You don't; we do. It's our agreement, leave it to us." If that does not work, get another facilitator.

- *They give the impression to one side or the other that they are not independent.* They always need to be independent and avoid being the messenger.

- *They make the error of breaking confidentiality as a method to build trust with another party.* If they break trust with one party, the other party will most likely believe the facilitator will break confidentiality with them as well.

- *They lose patience to get an agreement at any cost.* When the parties are very close to reaching agreement, that is when the facilitator has to be most careful and patient. People are almost euphoric and anxious and yet the deal still may go sour.
- *They show their despair and demonstrate that they feel that they cannot make it, that they are giving up.* They need to persevere—there is always a solution.

No matter how clever or intelligent the facilitator may be, sometimes things do not work out reasonably. Facilitation does not guarantee success; it just increases the probability of success.

If there is no external facilitator, the role still has to be filled by internal resources. In one company, the organizational development specialist was assigned to the negotiating process as the facilitator. The parties trusted that individual and accepted his facilitation. In other cases the facilitation roles rotate between the company and the union. That can work effectively with proper joint training for the negotiators and for the facilitators.

WHY THE LABEL "MUTUAL GAINS NEGOTIATIONS"?

"Mutual gains negotiations" can also be called integrative bargaining, principle bargaining, collaborative bargaining, best-practice bargaining, and interest-based bargaining. In this book the term "mutual gains negotiations" has been selected because it refers to the results to be achieved.

The emphasis should be on results; the sustaining characteristic of this process will be whether or not all parties experience mutual gain. The result is insufficient if the process is a success but a mutual gains agreement is not achieved. On the other hand, if parties use another process and the result is a mutual gains agreement, the result is a success.

What Should This Process Be Called When Parties Are Negotiating?

Labels are useful as a quick method to refer to something and for motivational purposes for new programs. But mutual gains negotiations is not a program; it is a new process, a new way of doing things to achieve a certain kind of result. Labeling the new approach to dispute resolution with a specific title such as "mutual gains negotiations" can create a barrier to successful implementation of the process.

At times the label has become a negotiating item. People may suggest that the parties should "do mutual gains negotiations" or even worse, "do MGN." In one negotiation, the parties used the label "mutual gains bargaining" to mean that if they could not resolve a problem by achieving mutual gains it would be taken off the agenda. The label in this case actually hurt the process. Of course, mutual gains refers to the total agreement, not necessarily the result of each and every problem.

In another negotiation, a company used the label "interest-based negotiating." They began referring to it as "IBN." Unfortunately, when some difficulties in negotiations arose, managers and union leaders began referring to the negotiations as "in bed negotiating." Immediately, this reinforced the difficulties they were having with the process. People began thinking that the new process was a trick that gave an advantage to the party who introduced it.

Organizations introducing other new initiatives have had similar experiences. The quality movement has suffered from the perception that "quality" means "head-count reductions." People see efficiency movements as threatening to job security. "Flexibility" as a label has been perceived as expanding management freedom at the expense of union freedom. The same kind of problem emerges in the labor relations arena.

The alternative is to not label the process. If you must call it something, use an innocuous term such as "effective negotiations" or "joint problem solving." One company chose to call it "customer-focused negotiations" to reflect the common interest of meeting the customers' needs as the essence of survival for both the company and the union. The alternative is a no-name approach, which will lead people to believe that the name is meaningless—and, in fact, it is meaningless.

When parties follow the process in a natural way without labeling it, they ask questions such as "You are making this kind of demand. Why do you want this?" Invariably, the response identifies what the other party thinks the problem is that led to that demand. From that new problem definition, the parties generate some creative ideas and alternative solutions emerge.

Whatever the parties decide to call the process, the name should not be a negotiated item. It should not be on the agenda to be dealt with as a serious political issue. Rather than label the process, just begin the process. This consists of knowing the problem, identifying the interests, exploring the facts, brainstorming solutions in a nonbinding manner, and then testing the quality of the solutions you are entertaining. Just do it!

SUMMARY

- Some of the steps in mutual gains negotiation addressed in this chapter are:
  - Make opening statements.
  - Confirm using the mutual gains negotiations process.
  - Develop negotiating principles among the parties.
  - Develop the full list of problems to be negotiated.
  - Set the timelines and locations for the negotiations.
- Mutual gains opening statements often have these characteristics:
  - Set the tone for mutual gains negotiations.

- – Emphasize the importance of not having status differences.
- – Express hope for the negotiations.
- The basic steps of the mutual gains process model are:
  1. Know and understand the problem.
  2. Discover creative solutions.
  3. Reach mutual gains agreement.
- The mutual gains bargaining process can be used when the issues lend themselves to collaborative problem solving. In other cases the parties may not have enough trust to discuss certain issues openly.
- Before exploring the problem, parties need to determine the negotiating principles.
- Perhaps the best way to have quality negotiating principles is for the parties to engage in joint training.
- Parties vary in the principles they consider and use in negotiations. The extent of the detail varies depending on the amount of trust between the parties. Some of the principles include honesty, following the mutual gains problem-solving process, dealing with the problems and not the personalities, reaching decisions by consensus, giving negotiators the authority to make a decision or a strong recommendation, and joint planning of confidentiality and communications.
- The most important part of the opening session is for parties to identify jointly the problems that will form the agenda for the negotiations.
- The order of the problems on the agenda is an important issue. The best way for parties to build trust in each other is to address the problems in the common interest first.

- After the parties have set the agenda, they can work out the specific logistics—location and the amount of time spent in actual negotiation.
- The ease with which parties are willing to use mutual gains negotiating varies depending on the nature of the problem.
- Many first-time mutual gains negotiators have found it useful to have external facilitation for their first attempt at using this new process.
- The following are characteristics of effective facilitators:
  - Fair, independent, neutral, trustworthy, and there to help both sides.
  - Keep the parties talking in a constructive way.
  - Have the sensitivity to call a time-out if the parties become aggressive.
  - Keep control if someone loses their temper.
  - Never become the go-between.
- The facilitator needs to be thoroughly knowledgeable about the situation in order to be a provocateur, asking the tough questions and ensuring the intellectual integrity of the process.
- These are some of the ways facilitators can be the problem:
  - Think they know the answers better than the negotiating parties do.
  - Give the impression to one side or the other that they are not independent.
  - Make the error of breaking confidentiality as a method to build trust with another party.
  - Lose patience to get an agreement at any cost.

- Show their despair and demonstrate that they feel that they cannot make it, that they are giving up.
- Labeling the new approach to dispute resolution with a specific title such as "mutual gains negotiations" can create a barrier to successful implementation of the process.
- Whatever the parties decide to call the process, the name should not be a negotiated item.

CHAPTER 6

Knowing and Understanding the Problem

A company and its union decided to engage in mutual gains negotiating. After developing the negotiating principles, they realized they needed external facilitation for at least their first experience with this new process. Ironically, paying the facilitators became the issue that almost sabotaged the parties' willingness to proceed. The parties agreed they would split the facilitator fees in half and that the union would repay their half after the completion of the contract. However, after the parties reached a tentative understanding, senior management, who was not part of the face-to-face negotiations, did not approve it. They wanted the union to pay monthly after they received each invoice.

The scene became explosive. The union accused management of bad-faith bargaining. Management responded that an agreement was not an agreement until it was signed. The parties needed facilitation desperately but were not able to decide how they would pay the facilitator. This clearly was an opportunity for the facilitator to offer some initial pro bono work to get things started.

After extensive deliberation and delay, the parties finally disclosed their real concerns. Management was concerned that as a condition to signing the collective agreement the union would demand that the facilitator's fee should be forgiven. Therefore, they wanted the union to make monthly payments. The union was concerned that the company negotiators did not have the authority to make decisions and this would make it difficult to continue mutual gains negotiations.

Once the parties were willing to spend time understanding the problem rather than presenting demands and counterdemands, they realized the problem was solvable. They concluded that the union would pay its 50 percent after the collective agreement was signed. The parties determined that if the union did not pay within a specified period of time, the company could take the money from union dues. They shook hands, signed a memorandum, and proceeded with mutual gains negotiating. The rough start was unnecessary, but it became a lesson that helped the parties recognize that bargaining could go wrong if they didn't explore interests.

While this is a somewhat humorous story, it is also a sad one. If the parties had been clear about their problem, the outcome would have been very different. It is essential for parties in a dispute to identify their problem precisely. The discussion of Phase 3 in the next two chapters explores mutual gains problem solving for each issue to be negotiated. This chapter explores the first three major components of mutual gains problem solving. These are:

1. Identify the common interests.
2. Clarify the known, unknown, and to-be-known facts.
3. Develop the joint problem statement.

IDENTIFY THE COMMON INTERESTS

A major distinction between classic problem solving and mutual gains negotiations is in the area of interests. Problem-solving models and the total quality movement operate under the assumption that all participants have the same interest, which is to resolve the problem in the wisest and simplest manner. These models do not regard emotions, personal agendas, motivations, fears, and concerns as particularly relevant to the problem-solving process.

In conflict situations, emotions and personal motivators are not only relevant but often the heart of the problem. Most conflicts result from different interests and motivators. Hence, in mutual gains negotiations, enhancing the relationship is an essential outcome of the process, while it is far less important in classic problem solving or quality initiatives.

At first glance, the purpose of exploring interests is to find the common interests on which to base problem-solving approaches. But this search process is not always enough to yield a common-interest solution. Independent interests are often relevant to a party, enhance understanding of the other party's concerns, and will not be submerged by the desire for commonality.

All interests need a voice in the mutual gains negotiation process. Those problems that reflect more common interests will be easier to solve than problems reflecting strong independent interests. Nevertheless, parties need to explore all problems with the real interests uncovered. As one leader said: "Start from where you are." If the separate interests are strong, parties should focus on how they can discover mutual gains solutions that meet both those separate interests and the common interests.

Parties Should Understand Their Own Interests

It is vital to the mutual gains negotiation process that parties explore their own interests. To identify their interests, they will probably have to engage in some serious soul-searching, asking themselves questions such as:

- What are our real needs and what motivates us to have those needs?
- What are our current concerns?
- What are our fears?

From these reflective questions, they will identify their interests. In some cases, this requires surveying their population to determine their motivators, concerns, and fears. Parties should be prepared to share them with their counterparts in the negotiation process.

Avoid Confusing Interests with Demands

When identifying interests, parties often make the error of confusing interests with demands. Interests are not demands or solutions in disguise. They are not the solution to the problem. They reflect the feelings, concerns, and fears that worry or excite the parties as they struggle with a particular problem.

Let's confirm the reader's understanding in a simple test. Identify which of the statements below are interests and which are solutions in disguise.[13]

_____ 1. We need a salary cap to control costs.

_____ 2. Our primary concern is for job security for our employees.

_____ 3. We need flexibility to better meet personal and family responsibilities.

_____ 4. We need to reduce our costs by 6 percent by laying off 100 workers.

_____ 5. We are concerned about the impact of new technology on our workers.

_____ 6. We want the right to contract out.

_____ 7. We need to go from three shifts to two shifts because of decreased customer demand.

_____ 8. We are concerned about the time it takes for complaints to be resolved through the grievance process.

Items 2, 3, 5, and 8 are interests. The others are demands for specific solutions and, when presented as interests, are really solutions in disguise. Items 1 and 4 would be interests if they said: "We are concerned about rising costs." Item 6 may be based on a cost interest, a productivity interest, or something else, but it is worded as a demand. Item 7 could reflect a concern for decreased customer demand and the reduction of the overall business.

Speculate about the Interests of Your Counterparts

In traditional negotiations, parties generate demands based on their own interests. In mutual gains negotiations, parties consider not only their own interests but their counterparts' interests as well. Their hope is to meet their own interests well and those of their counterparts adequately so that all parties experience mutual gain. The overlap of interests between the parties, referred to as the "common interests," is where mutual gains solutions are built.

Stephen Covey, in his best-selling book, *Seven Habits of Highly Effective People,* put this very well when he said, "First understand before being understood."[14] The challenge in any kind of planning process is to consider what the other side's interests are—even before considering your own. Before you convince yourself that your interests are the only interests, explore the other side to see the validity of their concerns.

In the mutual gains negotiations process, the purpose of thinking about your counterparts' interests is to be prepared to hear what they say in the actual exchange during negotiations. You are not expected to tell your counterparts what you believe are their interests. You may be mistaken and assume they have some particular interests when that is not true. In addition, they may identify certain interests that you did not even see as relevant to their situation. You may also identify some of their potential "land mine" interests (often highly personal or political interests), which if you articulate on their behalf may disable the entire process.

Examples of Separate Interests of Unions

Some interests are typically interests of the union and not of the company. These include:

- **Concern for erosion of job security and wage protection.** For many unions, this concern is the major issue in negotiations in these turbulent economic times. Some unions have had success in meeting the job security interest but often at the expense of reducing wage protection and/or increasing flexibility to assign work to the companies.

- **Enhancement of compensation, pensions, and benefits for membership.** This concern is a primary reason for the existence of unions. In almost every negotiation, the union tries to maximize the monetary package, while the company tries to limit it.

- **Concern for the erosion of the concept of seniority.** The concept of seniority is a fundamental belief of trade unionists. The belief is that a person who has worked for a company longer than another person should receive more money, have more job security, and have more say about what he or she does than someone with less time. Excellent performance beyond expectations is a management concept. Pay for all employees should be the same except for distinctions arising from seniority. Many companies do not view seniority as something of value. Their primary interest is in performance results, which should determine the compensation level and autonomy of employees.

- **Enhance the rights of union membership.** Many unions believe in the principle that "my freedom ends where your freedom begins." When freedoms conflict, one side offers solutions to abolish the system, while the other side wants to introduce further legislation and controls. That is why many unions look to contract negotiations as an opportunity to increase their legislated rights as documented in the collective agreement. They also resist giving the company more flexibility to assign work that will reduce the unionized employees' rights to know precisely what they will be doing on any given day.

- **Concern about the collective over the individual.** Unions are concerned about collective needs more than the needs of individuals. One example of this is unions' response to excessive overtime. They view overtime as a management strategy to replace full-time employees. If overtime is at the expense of hiring more people, the union will want companies to hire more employees to meet the collective need rather than benefit individuals with overtime pay.

- **Desire to expand bargaining units to include other workers.** Many unions have realized that they have more negotiating power if they represent a large employee base and if their membership includes employees who are crucial to the operations of the company. The implication is that unions often want to expand by certifying nonunionized employees and/or taking over responsibility to represent employees who are in other unions. A union's interest in increasing its membership is a major concern for companies and rival unions. When there are potential union raids, it is not uncommon for the trust between two unions to be significantly lower than the trust between union and management.

- **Survival of the union and reelection of the union leadership.** The union needs to preserve its own existence for the collective good. At times, that interest becomes an important concern in collective bargaining. In one situation, the union's interest in its own survival led it to agree that it would accept a major layoff in exchange for the company paying the lost union dues for the next three years. Although the parties ratified the agreement, it was extremely unpopular with the membership. They thought the extra money paid by the company should have gone to the severed employees or to the remaining employees in the company.

- **To be the representative to membership for communications.** Union and management often view the communication relationship with unionized employees differently. Unions see a linear relationship: Managers communicate to the union, and the union communicates to the membership. This approach is especially important to the unions during contract negotiations. Management sees a triangular relationship of management, union, and employees. This approach means management believes they can access their employees whenever they want and do not need to communicate through the union.

Examples of Separate Interests of Companies

Some interests are typical company interests rather than union interests. These include:

- **Concern with rising costs.** Costs are often the major concern for companies in negotiations. Labor represents a major part of the cost equation for companies. Any method to reduce labor costs (compensation, pension, and benefits) will increase profits and/or allow the company to pass the lower costs back to the customer.

- **Need for flexibility in work assignment.** Management believes they have the basic right to assign work and to create as big or as small a job as they want. They are concerned with any limit to their ability to operate their facility on an 8,760 hour basis. In other words, management believes they have the right to conduct business seven days a week and 24 hours a day if it is legal and if it adds to their ability to compete and meet customer needs.

- **Concern for skills obsolescence and the ability to learn.** Skills obsolescence and the ability to learn have become major problems for some companies. With the advent of computer technology, robotics, and so on, many skills that were useful in the workforce of the past are not necessary anymore. Employees with obsolete skills may not be learning new skills. At the same time they tend to be older and have more seniority and more job security. Skills obsolescence connected with the inability (or unwillingness) to learn new skills is a major barrier to modernization for many companies. This interest is sometimes a common interest of both companies and unions.

- **Concern for erosion of management rights.** Concern for the erosion of management rights to manage is more expensive than giving employees five cents more per hour. Management does not want to reduce management rights to writing because then they would be defined clearly. Management believes they should not ask for what they already have. Basically, they believe that everything not explicitly stated in the contract is a management right.

- **Desire to pay differentially based upon performance.** Most companies would much rather pay for performance than for seniority. Their only problem is that most companies have not figured out an effective system to measure performance or a pay system that works equally well in good and in bad economic times.

- **Not to negotiate grievances during contract negotiations.** Some unions attempt to negotiate grievances as part of the final stages of collective bargaining. Companies see the grievance process as separate from the collective bargaining process. In one situation the union negotiator demanded that the company give in on a grievance as a condition for the union to agree to a contract. The company spokesperson said: "I will take a strike over that principle." After they stared at each other for a few moments, the union spokesperson said: "It was worth a try."

- **Not to set precedents for other groups in other bargaining units.** Sometimes a company negotiates with many unions or many bargaining locals within a union at the same time. What they negotiate with one union becomes the precedent for negotiation with another union. The company is concerned about setting those precedents with particular emphasis on compensation, pension and benefits, time off, and working conditions. They are also concerned about agreeing to practices that will have implications for future decisions.

- **Need for direct communication access with employees.** Management views the supervisory-to-employee relationship as a natural communication access route. They feel this access route is available to them at any time.

- **Desire for no work stoppages.** The cost of the first few weeks of a strike to a company is far greater than it is for a union. The union membership starts worrying about a strike only after they miss their first paycheck. They sometimes enjoy the ability to flex their muscles and show the company they have the power to shut them down. For the company, the political and customer backlash from a brief strike or even the anticipation of a strike can be devastating. Sometimes it may mean that customers will take their business elsewhere, which will have a profound affect on the ability of the company to compete.

Obviously, the union and the company have numerous separate interests. The surprise will be the extent to which parties can find common interests on which to build creative solutions to problems.

Whose Interests Should Be of Concern to Us?

Negotiators are often surprised when they are asked to identify all the parties who may be called "stakeholders" in a negotiation. Stakeholders are the parties who have a very strong opinion about the results of the negotiations. They see themselves as the potential winners and losers. They will probably read the contract carefully or pay very close attention to it because of the effect it will have on them.

For the purpose of identifying interests, mutual gains negotiators need to be concerned primarily with the principal stakeholders. In most cases they are the company and the union, but sometimes they include specific employee groups and the customer. Exploring the interests of the customer is often helpful because it can uncover a number of very useful common interests.

There are many other stakeholders as well. They are important to consider before deciding upon a particular solution. The stakeholders include three groups:

- The winners.

- The losers, who you have agreed should lose (i.e., the competition).

- The accidental losers. They are the people who had nothing to do with the problem and yet they are suffering as a result of the decision. For example, a decision to resolve a problem with the part-time employees may be at the expense of the full-time employees. The full-timers are accidental losers.

Before determining a solution to a problem, consider the tough questions the stakeholders may ask that the negotiators will have to answer when they present the agreement. Parties should be able to answer those questions in the same way their counterparts will explain them when they communicate the agreement.

Here are some of the stakeholders identified in a wide variety of negotiations:

- **Union negotiators.** Among their interests are representing their membership, getting the best agreement, reelection, and union survival.

- **Company negotiators.** Their interests include representing management interests, getting the best agreement, promotion, and company survival.

- **Members of the union.** Union members may have many different interests depending upon the issue and whether they are new employees, employees near retirement, future employees, laid-off employees, retired employees, or others.

- **Board of directors and senior executives.** Some of their interests include shareholder value, cost, customer service, no work stoppage, and not losing control of the company.

- **Nonunion employees.** They will read the contract carefully to see what precedent is established for them by the union contract.

- **Other unions.** These include any other union local within or outside the company that may be looking for a precedent on which to make demands.

- **Shareholders.** Their principal interest is in company value.

- **Customers.** Their interest is in timeliness, quality, and cost. They can be accidental losers if negotiations do not consider their interests.

- **First-line supervisors and stewards.** As mentioned earlier, never close a deal that first-line supervisors and union representatives cannot administer. Ultimately they are the ones who are the point of contact and the ones who have to work on a day-to-day basis with contract administration even if there are industrial relations professionals within the organization.
- **Families of the employees.** They are concerned with issues such as security, quality of life, money, benefits, and pensions.
- **Media.** They often are most interested in unsuccessful negotiations. Win/lose cases make better theater.
- **Competitors.** They hope the company and union will publicly battle and reduce customer loyalty and shareholder value.
- **Distributors and suppliers.** They are interested in their customers' survival.
- **The community.** They need constant employment, community investment, and labor peace.
- **The national union.** It may have totally different interests than the local representatives, and this can be a source of internal union conflict.
- **Government and the regulators, if applicable.** Frequently, their concern is the protection of the public in the event of a work stoppage.

Identifying Someone's Interests When They Will Not Tell You What They Are

A challenge in mutual gains negotiations is how to identify your counterpart's or other stakeholders' interests if they will not tell you what they are. One method is to guess, which will have a low probability of being correct. Negotiators want to increase the probability that they can guess their counterparts' real interests correctly.

The most obvious and direct method is to find an opportunity before the negotiations to ask what their interests are. If that approach does not yield results, negotiators can use a number of other methods to increase the accuracy of their guesses:

- Explore your counterparts' past behavior and from that infer their current interests. The best predictor of future behavior is past behavior.
- Know your counterparts' history. Read documents such as their constitution and annual reports.
- Analyze grievances and see what have been the concerns of the past.
- Survey the union membership or the organization for field information and use this research to identify interests.
- Consider what is popular in the field at the present time.
- Look at other situations in which your counterparts have had an opportunity to act. What were their interests in that case and how do they affect the current situation?
- Consider the personal preferences of your counterpart negotiators. Personal preferences often play a role in identifying interests.
- Look at precedents.
- Perhaps establish a negotiations principle that no issue will be explored unless the parties tell why it is of interest to them.
- Ask your counterparts to critique your ideas. Listen to the areas they critique to identify their interests.

If you can anticipate your counterparts' interests with greater accuracy, then you will be able to plan strategies that can fit the expected common interests. This will expedite the process and enhance the overall effectiveness of the mutual gains negotiations process.

How to Discuss Interests in Mutual Gains Negotiating

During negotiations, both sides present their own interests even if they appear controversial. The objective for each side is to identify the other party's interests so that they can understand their motivators, concerns, and fears. This process requires active listening skills with special attention on the ability to listen, reflect, paraphrase, clarify, and summarize what was said to achieve understanding.

Explore the other party's interests; however, do not be so presumptuous as to tell them what you think their interests are. Assume that they have done their homework and that they are accurately reflecting what they want to tell you about their feelings, the problem, and their interests.

In one negotiation, one side suggested what they thought the other side's interests might be. Their suggestion was not on target. Because their counterparts seemed to be considering these interests, however, the other side accepted their misunderstanding as relevant and tried to see how they could use this information to their advantage in the future. In fact, it was essential to their case and resulted in a breakdown of trust.

A classic humorous legal story reflects this idea. An individual was charged for biting off someone's ear. When the prosecution's star witness was asked if he saw the person bite off the ear, the witness continually said no. The prosecution asked again, "Did you see him bite off the ear?" and the witness said no. After asking the question several times, the prosecution finally said, "I have no more questions."

The defense attorney was a rookie without much experience in cross-examination. In this situation, the defense attorney should not have risked asking the witness questions that might adversely affect his client's case. The obvious strategy would have been for the defense to say "I have no questions" and allow the witness to step down. Instead, the defense attorney could not hold back his impulse and asked one question. He said to the witness, "If you did not see him bite off the ear, then what are you doing here?" The witness, without a moment's hesitation, said, "I saw him spit it out."

Parties should speak for themselves about their own feelings and interests. Avoid asking a question to which you are unwilling to hear the answer or you may be encouraging them to "spit it out."

Developing Common Interests

To begin the process of identifying common interests, both parties develop their own lists of interests. Then they examine the lists and identify those that they have in common. Each party's list may stimulate interests that the other party has as well. For example, employee morale often appears on the union's list but not on the company's. Upon consideration, the company invariably agrees that morale is a common interest. Similarly, the customer often appears on the company's list but not the union's. The union also subsequently recognizes the customer as a common interest.

Generally, it is beneficial for parties to generate as many common interests as they can. The more they identify, the easier the mutual gains negotiation process will be. Classic common interests reflect the joint struggle against competitive forces over which both the union and the company may have little, if any, control.

To survive, both the company and union have four classic common interests known as the four Ps: Peace, People, Productivity, and Profit. As long as these interests are not at the expense of other interests, they are usually common interests. These common interests, as articulated by The Honourable Alan B. Gold, "are not only the employers' goals, they are basic, valid and in our system necessary trade union goals, without which there can be no decent working conditions, no job security, no pensions and no peace of mind for the workers, and little, if any, job satisfaction."[15]

Other examples of common interests include the following:

- Customer satisfaction.
- Job satisfaction.
- Meaningful work.
- Competent and trained employees.
- Competitiveness.
- Quality products and services.
- Reliability of products and services.
- Safe work environment.
- Effective communications.

If the parties identify interests and notice that all of them are common, a solution should be clear and evident very quickly. If not, parties may consider examining the interests that are not common to determine what is important to each of them. They may find that addressing their separate interests may be a potential secondary solution to resolve the dispute.

If the interests are all common, yet there is no agreement, another separate underlying interest probably exists. Sometimes the parties proceed through nonbinding creative idea generation, converge the ideas, and are still unable to reach a joint decision. Most often the blockage stems from some undisclosed interests. Further exploration of the interests will usually identify the source of the resistance. The resolution of the problem may then be within reach.

Consider Writing the Common Interests into the Contract

Some preambles to collective agreements include the intent of the new relationship and articulate the agreed-upon common interests. One major telecommunications company and one of its unions agreed to begin their contract with text that included the following:

There are substantial strengths within the Company and the Union which can be built on successfully. As the parties jointly face the challenges of the future, they share the following values:

- Customer focus.
- The overriding value of people as a resource.
- Quality and continuous improvement.
- A continuous learning environment.
- Union-management partnership.
- Employee diversity.
- Positive human interactions.[16]

Documentation of the common interests and values in the contract is a key to success in mutual gains negotiations. After successful mutual gains negotiations, the parties are usually ready to go public with their common interests. At that point it is most appropriate for them to discuss how they can reflect the beliefs in the contract.

CLARIFY THE KNOWN, UNKNOWN, AND TO-BE-KNOWN FACTS

Parties explore interests to reach understanding; they explore facts to achieve knowledge. Together, the interests and facts guide the parties to discover the joint problem and eventually to reach a wise and simple solution.

Facts are often presented after interests are discussed to help focus on the facts of greatest importance to your counterparts. Negotiators must communicate certain facts to each other so they will have the information necessary to discover a mutually agreeable solution to their problem. Therefore, it is essential that negotiators know what they should and should not communicate.

There are five categories of facts in mutual gains negotiations:

1. Facts known by both parties.
2. Unknown facts that are essential to the problem and need to be known.

3. Facts known by one party that will eventually be known to the other party.

4. Facts known by only one party that will never be known to the other party.

5. Guesses, deceptions, and lies disguised as facts.

The first three categories of facts—those known by both parties, the unknown, and facts known by one party that will eventually be known by the other party—must be communicated in negotiations. If parties do not communicate these facts, one of the parties inevitably feels tricked and the victim of bad-faith bargaining.

The fourth category is facts known by only one party. The other party will never know these facts unless the party with the facts reveals them. Parties have an option as to whether to communicate these types of facts.

The fifth category—guesses, deceptions, and lies disguised as facts—should never be communicated because they will destroy trust between the parties.

Category 1: Facts Known to Both Parties

If you were buying a house, facts such as location, the asking price, and any previous purchase prices of the house would be information known to both you and the seller. They would be some of the known facts.

Known facts are not your guesses about the facts. They do not reflect your interpretations of the facts. They are admissible evidence that can be put forth as actually having occurred. Therefore, parties communicate these facts to each other so that everyone will know them.

Some examples of known facts that parties might review are:

- The content of an article in the collective labor agreement, which is the parties' focus at the time.

- Any grievances that have resulted and how those grievances were resolved, if they were.
- Methods used by other organizations to deal with the problems being addressed in the current negotiations.

Category 2: Unknown Facts That Are Essential to the Problem and Need to Be Known

In the house-purchasing example, assume the parties choose to close the purchase without the support of real estate agents. They may be unfamiliar with the documentation required to consummate the deal. Eventually, all parties will know if there are errors in the documentation. The parties must explore and understand these facts and include them in the purchasing process.

In labor-management negotiations, these kinds of facts appear as well. In one situation, the company and the union were attempting to resolve a complex problem that was related to pensions. The company anticipated extreme cost pressures as a result of an aging workforce, and the union agreed to explore methods to resolve the problem.

Category 2 facts were evident immediately. The parties needed more knowledge about pensions. They brought in experts to explain alternatives, precedents, and benchmarks. Internal pension resources explained the current system in extensive detail to both parties. As the parties explored alternative solutions, specific content experts were brought into the negotiations to help validate their recommendations and ensure they were legal. Discovering the unknown information was essential to the problem-solving process and helped the parties generate a solution that they believed achieved mutual gain.

This category of facts can also lead to a potential trap as well. One negotiator called it the search for the "optimum of ignorance." When are enough facts about a problem actually enough? Parties can study some topics to death, make them unnecessarily complex, and use them as a delay tactic through the fact collection process.

A well-known legal story illustrates this dilemma. A young lawyer was involved in a fairly simple case, but for one reason or another, was making it more and more complicated as time went by. Finally, when the judge was clearly beginning to show signs of impatience, the lawyer, in an effort to smooth things over, asked: "I must trust your lordship is following me?" To which the judge replied: "I am following you very well, but pray, where are we going?"

The "optimum of ignorance" is the minimum number of facts required to make an informed, wise, and simple decision. There are always opportunities to learn more and to make the problem more complex. On occasion it will be appropriate to have a joint union-management "sidebar" group research the topic on behalf of the negotiators and present a report on the facts discovered about the problem. For complex problems, the parties should discuss how much they need to know so that they can resolve a mutual gains problem efficiently.

The total quality movement is particularly strong in this kind of fact exploration and research. Analyses of cause and effect, Pareto diagrams, fishbone diagrams, and others are excellent tools to identify the unknown facts about a problem and can be used by the union and company negotiators. This book will not explore these tools because they are widely discussed in other books.

Category 3: Facts Known by One Party That Will Eventually Be Known to the Other Party

Consider the house-purchasing example once again. Assume the seller has had a problem with flooding in the basement. The seller has some cosmetic structural work done, but it does not resolve the problem. The buyer has the structure, heating, insulation, and roof inspected, and the building inspector does not detect the flood damage. The seller does not reveal this fact about the house to the buyer. Only after signing the contract does the buyer find that the house has basement floods and that the owner did not tell him.

It is the seller's responsibility to communicate that there is a serious problem. This information is a fact that should be known to both parties. Hiding it is considered bad-faith bargaining. Since it can be verified that flooding occurred, the coverup is inappropriate and constitutes a "gotcha deal."

What is a "gotcha deal"? It is a deal made by a deceptive negotiator, who withholds essential information that will eventually be known—that he knew about during negotiations. Essentially, the negotiator says, "I gotcha [got you] now where I want you." It is an example of bad-faith bargaining.

The "gotcha deal" generates responses similar to the one we described earlier in which the dissatisfied party with no choice becomes a terrorist. In one case a company representative was deceptive, which resulted in a "gotcha deal." The union negotiator grieved based on bad-faith bargaining and nondisclosure of the facts. The union received retribution through the legal system, and the company released the management "gotcha dealer."

Some facts that are known to one party during negotiations may become known to the other party eventually, perhaps only after the negotiations. They may be facts about decisions one of the parties made prior to the negotiations about actions it will take afterwards. If the party who has the information chooses not to reveal the facts, the other party will feel tricked when learning that the facts were withheld.

This is a controversial area of communicating facts that often generates resistance from parties. It is essential for parties to sustain trust between each other and avoid "gotcha deals." Parties should communicate facts that will be known to the other party after the negotiation process.

An excellent example of how trust is destroyed when this type of information is withheld is the negotiation that occurred between the leadership of a government and its public service unions. The government announced that it needed $2 billion to reduce its deficit. The government reported that it will shut down for 12 days during the year to reduce the deficit. It gave the unions three months to negotiate alternate ways to raise the $2 billion.

A tremendous uproar arose because of the threat to the unions. Nevertheless, strong bargaining occurred, and they reached agreements to avoid the 12-day shutdown and to generate the necessary revenue. They struck a deal by the target date, and there was a great sigh of relief. The belief was that there would be some safety for the unions, and the budget also would be reduced by $2 billion.

Shortly after the negotiations, the leadership of the government announced it would shut down the government for three successive Fridays. The government had not announced this action during the negotiations. The unions responded with intense anger, which resulted in part from what appeared to some union leaders as a "gotcha deal." The "gotcha deal" was perceived as follows:

- The government must have known at the time they made their decision to shut down the government for 12 days that it was going to take 3 additional days.

- If the government had wanted to take 15 days in total, it should have revealed this from the beginning of the negotiations.

The relationship between the union and the government was strained. It was difficult enough to negotiate the $2 billion, but the perception that the government had withheld information caused even greater problems.

Adding to the problem was the arbitrator's ruling that the government would not be permitted to shut down for an additional three days. They had to proceed with the deal as constructed by the target date with the union: either to shut down for 12 days or use the replacement strategies the union and the government had negotiated.

The credibility and trust of the government with the unions were destroyed in part because they appeared to have withheld facts that the union would know after the negotiations. The perception of a "gotcha deal" backfired on the government.

A core principle in communicating the facts is to avoid a "gotcha deal." In communicating facts, keep in mind that the "need to know" the facts is in the eyes of the beholder. If a party believes it is deceived in the process of negotiation, all of the trust built through the mutual gains process can be destroyed. Parties must communicate the third category of facts to avoid that loss of trust.

In mutual gains negotiations, you are not negotiating to get just a deal but rather a deal you can live by. Reaching an agreement is not the end but the beginning. If, after you reach agreement, you destroy the spirit of the agreement by having the other party believe you tricked them into it by not revealing certain information, then you have generated a "gotcha deal." Your perceived lack of honesty will cause you to fall out of trust and destroy the relationship. The other party will eventually find an opportunity to get back at you in some way.

In mutual gains negotiations, the parties identify all the known, the essential unknown, and to-be-known facts that need to be communicated about a problem. They ensure that everyone knows the same facts and assume nothing, thereby avoiding a "gotcha deal."

Category 4: Facts Known by Only One Party That Will Never Be Known to the Other Party

In the house-purchasing example, facts known only to one party include how much money the buyer has to spend, how little money the seller is willing to accept, and whether the buyer and seller like each other. These facts are not communicated because the seller assumes he will get more than his bottom line and the buyer assumes he will pay less than his maximum price.

In union-management negotiations, unless a party actually communicates these kinds of facts, they will never be known to the other party. Two examples of information known only to one party are:

- What the parties feel about each other.

- A party's bottom line, or the point beyond which the party shifts gears and resorts to power. Usually people want to get more than their bottom line, so they rarely disclose it. You can be quite sure that the other party will rarely obtain this information.

One of the recurrent struggles in mutual gains negotiating is the extent to which the parties must disclose all their facts, open their books, and communicate everything. They ask: "What is the minimum number of facts we must communicate to be consistent with mutual gains negotiating?" The answer is: You communicate all the facts your counterpart needs to know to avoid a "gotcha deal."

Consider the customer-supplier relationship. Customers expect to be told the known, the unknown, and the to-be-known facts (Categories 1 to 3) when purchasing a product or service. They do not expect you to tell them if you have internal problems that do not affect the quality of the product or service. Customers do not expect to know your cost structure or your profit margins either. The supplier does not expect to know if there are other suppliers or how much money the customer has to spend. Each party just wants a fair price for the product or service.

In mutual gains negotiations, the analysis takes a similar direction. Although your counterparts would like to know every-thing, as the source of the facts you need to determine what they need to know to work through the problem. As a minimum standard, the facts in Categories 1 to 3 are all your counterpart needs to know to avoid the "gotcha deal." If Category 4 facts never become known to your counterparts, then the standard of mutual gains negotiations has been met. Communicating Cat-egory 4 facts is an option for the party with that knowledge.

However, if you do decide not to communicate Category 4 information during a negotiation, you have to be sure to avoid a "gotcha deal" by never communicating that information. For example, in one negotiation the union received a 3 percent in-crease. After the negotiations, the management negotiator re-vealed to the union spokesperson that he had been willing to give a 5 percent increase and laughed at the union spokesperson. Feeling that he was the victim of a "gotcha deal," the union spokesperson was extremely angry. The management negotiator should not have disclosed his information.

On the other hand, it is amazing how disclosure of Category 4 facts to the other party during negotiations enhances the trust that people feel for each other. Trust begets trust. If you trust others with information known only to you, they tend to respond by trusting you with their Category 4 information. With that kind of trusting relationship, you will be able to negotiate mutual gains agreements, reflect the needs and interests of your constituencies, and manage the collective labor agreement throughout its term.

Category 5: Guesses, Deceptions, and Lies Disguised as Facts

Negotiators should never communicate guesses as if they were facts. Eventually, the other party finds out that the so-called facts were actually just guesses and feels the victim of a "gotcha deal." Sometimes parties believe the information they have is true but they are not certain. If they have some doubt about the information, they should say so. If they pass the guess off as fact and it is proven to be less than totally true, they will fall out of trust with the other party.

The extent to which lying actually takes place in most negotiations may surprise some readers. Often parties fabricate excuses for a demand to make the other side think the demand is something they would want as well. Sometimes the excuses are lies. The negotiators concoct the story because information is lacking or because what they know about the case would never convince the other side. Therefore, they feel they have to contrive a better case in order to convince the other party that their demand is justifiable.

When negotiators lie, they are committing perjury. Lying is totally unacceptable in negotiations. If a party is discovered lying or operating in a deceptive way, the other party feels betrayed and any trust developed between the two is destroyed. It takes a tremendous amount of effort to regain the relationship that is sabotaged by lies and deceit.

In a recent negotiation, a union representative contrived a story to justify a claim. The company spokesperson asked the union representative one question each day, which forced the union representative to embellish the story. By the seventh day of isolated questioning, the company spokesperson posed a question to which the only response possible was "I lied."

The union representative did not respond. For 10 minutes, everyone at the table was silent. No one talked; no one moved. It seemed as if no one breathed. After 10 minutes, the union spokesperson said, "I think we should take a break."

Everyone left the room. In the company's caucus room, the company spokesperson told his team that the silence had been vital to ensure that the deception would be removed from the negotiations process. Interestingly, on the union side, the spokesperson was grateful that the inappropriate behavior of one of his negotiators was stopped because he was unable to stop it himself. The parties never referred to that incident again during the negotiations. They were able to proceed because of this dramatic move.

Typically, people respond to deception and lies by not telling the other person that they know about the lies. One person believes he has successfully deceived the other party, while the other party is waiting for the opportunity to disclose the liar's lack of trustworthiness.

It is hard enough to remember the truth correctly. It's almost impossible to remember all the lies. Even guesses passed off as facts are hard to remember. Lying is a very bad strategy. People should say nothing rather than lie.

Presentation of Facts during Negotiations

When negotiations begin, the company and the union present the generic facts that are known and to-be-known and that are relevant to the overall negotiations. They record these facts on flip charts and then display them on the walls throughout the negotiations.

As known and to-be-known facts emerge throughout the process, the parties add them to that list of facts. The facts that are true for one problem are true for the next problem as well. They do not lose their validity as the parties consider other problems, and they may be relevant when the parties consider other issues later.

The parties record on flip charts the facts that are pertinent to each problem. They use the recorded facts as the foundation on which to build common interests, brainstorm solutions, and generate the most effective solution to the overall problem.

On occasion, parties may want to distribute supportive written documentation. Typically, the documentation is given out at the time of the presentation or immediately afterwards. The decision about when to distribute the documentation is based on the desire to create the greatest comprehension of the presentation. It is not meant to be a manipulative strategy by the presenter. If the audience wants the documentation when it is presented rather than afterwards, the presenter would be wise to meet that request and not make an issue of it.

After the parties explore their interests and identify those they have in common, they consider the specific facts of each problem. Next, they develop the joint problem statement.

DEVELOP THE JOINT PROBLEM STATEMENT

A wise mediator was called in to help two disputing parties. The parties were presenting demands to each other in an aggressive fashion and the conflict was escalating. The mediator realized that working on the demands would only accentuate the differences and would be a fruitless approach. Rather, he said: "If you can not agree on the answers, can you at least agree on the question?"

The mediator asked the disputants to independently identify the question for which their demand functioned as the solution. Not surprisingly, the questions each of the disputants developed were not the same. Their challenge was to agree to the question on which they would work. Eventually they identified the joint problem and found a solution that achieved mutual gains.

The joint problem statement can emerge by working backwards as in the mediation case, although it is a technique that requires considerable finesse and skill. A more direct approach is to build to the problem statement by understanding the common interests, knowing the facts, and then developing the joint problem statement.

Never Mind the Solution . . . What's the Question?

A company decided to introduce a new computerized technology into its communication system. The new technology required employees to have advanced spatial reasoning and visual acuity. The company decided to have an open competition for the jobs and required specific testing as part of the selection process. Employees with the skills required for the new technology would be paid more than those whose jobs were similar but required a lower level of technology.

The company justified the open competition based upon the collective agreement, which specified that any employee could apply for a new job. The union was very concerned that younger employees would leapfrog over older and more senior employees to get the new and better paying jobs. They also believed that the job was simply an extension of the older job and that seniority should be the basis for the selection process.

The problem escalated until the parties decided to apply mutual gains negotiating to the case. A joint union-management team was sent to a mutual gains negotiations seminar with the explicit instruction to try using that approach after they completed the workshop.

After the workshop, they discussed the negotiation principles, determined each other's interests, and reviewed all the facts. They identified common interests, which included the customer, speed to market, leadership in technology application, productivity improvements, employee morale, union-management peace, and support of the collective labor agreement.

Next, they tackled the joint problem statement. They reviewed the method of developing problem statements they learned during the workshop. They realized the importance of stating the problem as a question. If they could agree on the question, they were much more likely to emerge from the negotiations with a solution that provided a clear answer.

These are the specific criteria for developing a problem statement into a question. The problem statement should have these characteristics:

- **Open-ended.** The questions need to lead to multiple responses through the brainstorming process. Therefore, the questions must be open-ended, those that you cannot answer with a simple yes or no response. "How" statements are preferred. The parties in our example decided to start their problem statement with, "How can we use the new technology effectively?"

- **Balanced.** A balanced question reflects the dilemma in the problem. It most often can be found in two common interests that are competing with each other. In this case, the common interests of labor-management peace were in conflict with productivity improvements. The parties decided to include those two common interests in the question. It now reads: "How can we use the new technology effectively so that it ensures labor-management peace and productivity improvements?"

- **Keep it positive.** It is preferable to word the question positively rather than negatively. For example, it is better to say, "How can we ensure the integrity of the collective bargaining unit within which the employees work?" rather than "How can we not erode the integrity of the collective bargaining unit within which the employees work?"

- **Not a leading question.** It was earlier stated that an interest should not be a solution in disguise. Similarly, a problem statement should not be a leading question that forces people to identify a specific solution. A leading question would be, "How can we ensure that senior employees will be the only ones to do the jobs?" This question requires a specific answer that one of the parties hopes to achieve but that is not in the common interest. The two parties need to agree to a question that reflects the perspective of both parties.

- **Focused.** It is very easy to generalize the problem statement to flexibility, cost, job security, seniority, wages, benefits, pensions, and so on. The more parties focus on the question they want to resolve, the easier it will be for them to brainstorm solutions related specifically to that question. In our example, the parties' problem statement could have been, "How can we implement new technologies into the company?" Although that is a valid question, it is much broader than the challenge before the negotiating parties. If their solution has precedent-setting potential after they conclude an agreement on this problem, then they could address the general question as the follow-up issue.

- **Easily understood.** All the negotiators should understand the joint problem statement easily. Eventually, the question may be part of the communication vehicle the parties use to explain the solution to the membership and management. The easier the question is to understand, the simpler the communication process will be. The question should set the tone for the simplicity of the problem by the fact that it is understandable.

At the outset of negotiations, the parties come to an agreement on the agenda of problem statements. They sequence the problems from those that can easily be expressed as a joint problem to those that appear to be a problem for only one party. When they start negotiating each problem statement, they review the information according to what they consider the problem statement to be and what they think the questions about the problem statement are.

Many negotiators find it difficult to generate questions. They have trouble identifying the real problem. In one case the facilitator challenged the negotiators by saying that if they could not find the question, perhaps there was no problem. When confronted this way, the negotiating parties worked harder at thinking through the problem and generating a balanced and meaningful problem statement.

The process of generating problem statements eliminates placing demands on the table that state what the parties want. The demands promote an either/or response. Either the other party says "yes" or it says "no." A demand provides the specific terms and conditions as to what a party will and will not do.

By making demands, parties limit the scope of choice and ultimately the ability to reach mutual gains solutions. By generating effective problem statements, the parties gain a better understanding of the core issue. This makes it easier to come up with effective mutual gains solutions that are wise and simple and that enhance the relationships between the parties.

SUMMARY

- This chapter explores the first three major components of mutual gains problem solving. These are:
  1. Identify the common interests.
  2. Clarify the known, unknown, and to-be-known facts.
  3. Develop the joint problem statement.

- A major distinction between classic problem solving and mutual gains negotiations is in the area of interests. In traditional negotiations, parties generate demands based on their own interests. In mutual gains negotiations, parties consider not only their own interests but their counterparts' interests as well.

- It is vital to the mutual gains negotiation process that parties explore their own interests. Parties should be prepared to share them with their counterparts in the negotiation process.

- When identifying interests, parties often make the error of confusing interests with demands.

- In the mutual gains negotiations process, the purpose of thinking about your counterparts' interests is to be prepared to hear what they say in the actual exchange during negotiations.

- Some interests are typically union rather than company interests. These include:

  - Concern for erosion of job security and wage protection.

  - Enhancement of compensation, pensions, and benefits for membership.

  - Concern for the erosion of the concept of seniority.

  - Enhancement of the rights of union membership.

  - Concern about the collective over the individual.

  - Desire to expand bargaining units to include other workers.

  - Survival of the union and reelection of the union leadership.

  - Being the representative to membership for communications.

- Some interests are typical company rather than union interests. Some of these include:
  - Concern with rising costs.
  - Need for flexibility in work assignment.
  - Concern for skills obsolescence and the ability to learn.
  - Concern for erosion of management rights.
  - Desire to pay differentially based upon performance.
  - Not to negotiate grievances during contract negotiations.
  - Not to set precedents for other groups in other bargaining units.
  - Need for direct communication access with employees.
  - Desire for no work stoppages.
- "Stakeholders" are the parties who have a very strong opinion about the results of the negotiations. They see themselves as potential winners or losers. They will probably read the contract carefully or pay very close attention to it because of the effect it will have on them.
- For the purposes of identifying interests, the mutual gains negotiators need to be concerned with the principal stakeholders only. In most cases they are the company and the union but sometimes include specific employee groups and the customer.
- Stakeholders can be categorized in one of three groups:
  1. The winners.
  2. The losers who you have agreed should lose (i.e., the competition).
  3. The accidental losers.

- A challenge in mutual gains negotiations is how to identify your counterpart's or other stakeholders' interests if they will not tell you what they are.
- During mutual gains negotiations, each side presents its own interests even if they appear controversial.
- To begin the process of identifying common interests, both parties develop their own lists of interests. Then they examine the lists and identify those they have in common.
- To survive, both the company and union have four classic common interests known as the four Ps: Peace, People, Productivity, and Profit. As long as these interests are not at the expense of other interests, they are usually common interests.
- Documentation of common interests in the contract is a key success factor in mutual gains negotiations.
- There are five categories of facts in mutual gains negotiations:
  1. Facts known by both parties.
  2. Unknown facts that are essential to the problem and need to be known.
  3. Facts known by one party that will eventually be known to the other party.
  4. Facts known by only one party that will never be known to the other party.
  5. Guesses, deceptions, and lies disguised as facts.
- The first three categories of facts must be communicated in negotiations. The fourth category of facts is known by only one party. Parties have an option as to whether to communicate these types of facts. The fifth category should never be communicated because it will destroy trust between the parties.

- A "gotcha deal" is one made by a negotiator who withholds essential information that will eventually be known, that he knew about during the negotiation. It is an example of bad-faith bargaining.

- It is essential for parties to sustain trust between each other and avoid "gotcha deals." Parties should communicate facts during negotiations that will be known by the other party after the negotiation process.

- In mutual gains negotiations, you are not negotiating just to get an agreement but rather an agreement you can live by.

- There are specific criteria for developing a joint problem statement into a question. The questions should be:
  - Open-ended.
  - Balanced.
  - Positive.
  - Not a leading question.
  - Focused.
  - Easily understood.

- The process of generating joint problem statements eliminates placing demands on the table that state what the parties want.

CHAPTER 7

Discovering Creative Solutions

A distinct advantage of the mutual gains negotiations process is that the parties explore the problems and potential solutions together. After they get inside the problems and explore creative solutions that are wise and simple, they then select solutions they prefer based upon common and separate interests.

The negotiations described in this book have in common the discovery of creative solutions. Because most problems are not simple, creativity is essential to mutual gains negotiations. Some problems may even be dilemmas that have been the subject of adversarial discussions for a long time. Joint creative thinking is often the missing variable that parties need to resolve a dilemma.

Mutual gains negotiating generates new and inventive solutions that enhance the ability of parties to resolve problems and achieve union-management peace. This chapter describes a method that helps parties identify the wisest and simplest mutual gains solutions to a problem.

In adversarial negotiations parties often trade wins and losses; they trade victory on one problem for a loss on a second, often unrelated problem. They do very little joint discovery or show little creativity within a problem when they use adversarial negotiating They begin and end with solutions and countersolutions, demands and counterdemands. In mutual gains negotiations, however, parties make every attempt to resolve problems directly rather than trade wins and losses.

Adversarial negotiations skip most of the preliminary steps described in Chapter 6. The result is that the parties have no opportunity to explore creative solutions or to explore the problems in depth. Instead, they trade solutions between issues rather than resolve problems directly. Almost all solutions in adversarial negotiations are based on trade-offs of one problem for another.

EXAMPLES OF MUTUAL GAINS CREATIVE SOLUTIONS

The following creative solutions to problems demonstrate some of the potential of the mutual gains process.

• Case: In Chapter 6 (p. 145) an example is given of a company that positioned a new technology role as a new job, which meant that the jobs would be filled through an open selection process. The union's position was that it was an existing job and seniority should apply. This problem was resolved by inviting all employees to apply for the job if they so desired. Training was offered to candidates based on seniority. After training, candidates were tested on the new technology directly. When all the positions were filled based on seniority and capability, the company discontinued the training.

• Case: A company had a complicated grievance process that always seemed to end up in arbitration. The parties agreed to two actions to simplify the process. First, if an employee had a grievance, the foreman and steward conducted a joint meeting with the employee. The purpose of the meeting was to focus on knowing and understanding the problem, not on solutions. This joint meeting reduced spurious grievances because the employee had to face both the union representative and the first-line supervisor. In addition, the parties resolved many cases once the facts and interests were clarified. Secondly, the parties decided to engage a private external case manager who used mutual gains problem-solving processes to try to help resolve the problem before proceeding to arbitration.

Parties can discover 18th camel solutions if they are willing to look together for them. The real benefit of mutual gains negotiations is the joint discovery process. By generating nonbinding creative ideas and discovering creative solutions, the parties find wise, simple, and relationship-enhancing solutions that contribute to labor-management peace.

NONBINDING CREATIVE IDEA GENERATION

During a problem-solving session, a manager said, "How can I be creative if everything I say is written down?" He expressed what most people would feel if they were held accountable for everything they said in a brainstorming session.

Negotiators can resolve this dilemma by agreeing to nonbinding brainstorming. In mutual gains negotiations, "nonbinding" is taken seriously. Parties consider any ideas (solutions or parts of solutions to the problem) that come to their minds. Those ideas are written on flip charts, and each chart is titled "nonbinding." At the end of the process, the parties hold a ceremony and rip up the charts to demonstrate that they will not be used again. In one negotiation, the parties included in the negotiation principles a statement saying that the documents, charts, and notes would be destroyed in a ceremonial burning after the negotiations or if and when either side decides not to proceed with this process.

HOW TO GET CREATIVE

Most people have the ability to be creative; they just do not express their creativity in negotiations. However, when people realize that the brainstorming process will be nonbinding, they are willing to explore and create 18th camel solutions.

This section describes a strategy for enhancing creativity that can be used in the mutual gains approach. It provides examples to illustrate how the strategy works and considers how the principles can be applied.

Challenge Assumptions

Chapter 3 considers the issue of trust. Trust or mistrust is based on assumptions. To be creative, parties must challenge, reevaluate, and often alter those assumptions.

As a result of their experience, most people have developed assumptions that are helpful most of the time. Without these assumptions, they would have to reevaluate every situation that required a decision, which would be a lengthy process.

When people are in conflict with others, however, the assumptions that have helped them the most in the past often lead them to resist new ideas and obstruct problem resolution. To generate creative responses, people need to break away from preconceived assumptions and consider alternatives.

The following simple exercise shows how people sometimes make assumptions. Ask a colleague to participate in an addition problem. Read out loud the numbers below and ask your colleague to complete the addition for each line.

-1,000
-add 40
-add 1,000
-add 30
-add 1,000
-add 20
-add 1,000
-add 10

What is their answer? Most people say 5,000. Some say 4,100, and others will have an alternative response. The correct answer is 4,100. Most people do the addition incorrectly not because they can't add but because of the way they respond when they add these numbers. They get into a rhythm of thinking that leads them to believe that 4,090 plus 10 is equal to 5,000 instead of 4,100. It sounds better, it feels better, and it seems right. On the other hand, some people are not comfortable with 4,100. In some cases, they even produce a number other than 5,000 or 4,100 because they know something is wrong, but they do not know the right answer.

Consider another example of how people make assumptions. In this example, take a sheet of paper and write the words "red," "blue," "green," and "orange" in colors that are different from the actual words. For example, you might write the word "red" with a green pen and the word "blue" with a red pen.

Next, ask a colleague to read these words. They do not have any problem reading the words. But when you ask them to tell you the colors used to write each of the words, they hesitate. This is because the spelling of the word is dominant, and it is not easy to break out of the assumption that the color and the spelling of the word will match.

In many negotiations, people operate under the assumption that their perspective is the only perspective and that the other party's interests are irrelevant. They generate solutions based on their own interests rather than trying to generate solutions based on the common interests. They assume that the only standards that are relevant are those that support their position, and they are blind to what the other side is actually saying. An important element in this creative process is for parties to move beyond those assumptions and consider alternatives that they may not have considered before.

Go Backwards

Most people solve problems through linear thinking. In mutual gains negotiations, a certain amount of linear thinking is useful.

For example, negotiators need to know and understand a problem before attempting to discover creative solutions. However, negotiators can work through the steps of identifying the interests, exploring facts, and identifying problems in any order. Rather than identifying interests first, they may start by exploring the facts; next, clarifying the problem; and then identifying interests. Alternatively, negotiators might start with problems, explore facts, and then identify interests.

Creative people often look for solutions to problems by thinking from a different perspective. Rather than moving forward, they may start at the end and go backwards. They recognize there is less resistance when they move in the opposite direction because the unknowns are behind rather than before them.

Consider the design of mazes and how people try to complete them. Most people work through mazes from the beginning to the end. Of course, mazes are designed to be confusing, forcing you to make many choices as you proceed from the beginning in your quest to reach the end. But when you work backwards, you have almost no choices to make because mazes are not designed to be complex from the end to the beginning.

Another example is how people read books. Unfortunately, most people read business books the way they read novels, from beginning to end. Most business books, however, are easier to read working backward from the conclusion to the preface. The last chapter of many business books tells the reader how to apply the model. Therefore, it makes sense to start with this chapter, since it might be the most interesting part of the book. The next chapters discuss the core model. Readers want to read them after they know how the model can be applied. Finally, the first few sections talk about the history and why it is necessary to use the book's approach. Because this portion of the book is often more conceptual, some readers may have little interest in it.

This book provides an example of this point. It ends with the vision of how to get beyond the walls of conflict from which the title of the book is taken. The specific methods to achieve union–management peace are discussed in the chapters just before the last chapter. The first few chapters of this book are conceptual and may not be of interest to those who are reading this book only for application.

In negotiations, one creative approach is to think from the end to the beginning of a problem by considering what the end state would look like if the problem were resolved. Next, the parties consider the steps that lead to that end state. Then they work backwards step by step until they reach the problem.

Parties can use a similar process when brainstorming. Ironically, many people believe there is only one way to brainstorm— generate a long list of ideas and then cluster them into meaningful categories. Sometimes, however, it is better to do "reverse brainstorming"—start with the categories you know will be essential to the solution and then brainstorm within the categories. If the parties know and agree to the categories, then they can begin with them and build creative ideas within each of the subareas. They should do what works, whether they go forward or backward or begin somewhere in the middle of the problem.

The principle is to find the path of least resistance. If it is easier to generate ideas by going backward or moving from the inside to the outside, or even by going forward, then do what works. Varying the process will not only help the parties generate many ideas, it will also make the negotiations more interesting and compelling to them.

Change the Access Routes to the Problem

A technique creative people often use is to consider the access routes, or the various angles from which they can enter a problem in order to solve it. The challenge is to consider as many access routes to a problem as possible and to see which one offers the path of least resistance to an effective negotiated solution.

To illustrate access routes, assume you are trying to schedule a tennis tournament for 87 singles players. A player who wins a match moves on until one player is the final winner. You have to schedule court times for all the matches. How many court times will be required?

Most people think that you start with 43 players against 43 players, so you have a minimum of 43 matches. Of course, you have the complication of the "bye." This is the position of a player who draws no opponent for the first round in a tournament and so advances to the next round without playing. Most people then add court times as the winners continue playing each other. The exercise is complicated and requires perseverance to identify the total number of matches required.

The most common access route to resolving this problem, but not the most useful one, is that whoever wins moves on. But if you change the access route from "whoever wins" to "whoever loses," the problem becomes simple. If you have 87 players, then you need 86 losers. That means you need 86 court times, so the answer is 86. Exploring alternative access routes and choosing the one of least resistance simplifies the entire problem, and new and inventive solutions become apparent.

In negotiations, parties may be trying to solve a working-condition problem. If, instead, they look at the problem from another access route such as money, the problem may be more easily resolved. What is the financial value of the change in the working condition to the union or to the company? By considering the problem from that vantage point, the parties may make some discoveries about the value of the change in working conditions. Perhaps some creative solutions they have not yet explored may become evident.

In fact, all negotiations problems can be reinterpreted as monetary issues. Parties then can define the cost of each problem as well as of the entire agreement. In one negotiation, for example, employees resisted working on weekends. Management needed weekend workers and were considering hiring contract workers for that purpose. The union was concerned about the precedent that would be established if the company hired contract workers for jobs that full-time employees were not willing to do although they had the ability to do them.

By redefining the problem in monetary terms, management was able to determine the real value of that flexibility and reflect that value in the overall compensation package for unionized employees. Contracting out was avoided, weekend work was done at special rates, and union-management peace was restored.

In another situation, a union and management were caught in the middle of a very complex sexual harassment case. Both the union and management wanted to reduce the trauma of investigating the situation, the likelihood of a lawsuit, and their potential liability if a lawsuit occurred. They recognized that an alternative access route to collect data would be in their common interest. They decided to share expenses to engage a jointly selected neutral third party to act in confidence, show no favoritism, and report on what happened.

Explore the Extremes

Sometimes solving a problem is easier if the parties can recognize the extremes of the solution. To break out of a pattern that is creating a dysfunctional negotiation process, it may work to go to the extreme. The parties try to find the point beyond which no one would consider the solution and the point within the problem that no one would consider a viable solution. Once the parameters are established, the parties may be able to work more effectively to achieve a reasonable solution to the problem.

Try It Another Way

A colleague of mine who works with children with Down's syndrome says that when the children are frustrated, they are trained to "try it another way." These words of wisdom are as helpful for the general population as well as for those who have disabilities. The general population often forgets to follow this advice.

George Will once indicated that he views people in North America as digging a very deep ditch economically, politically, and culturally. As they are inside this ditch, the only strategy they can think of is to continue to dig deeper. The message is that we have to try it another way. Creative people consistently recognize that if they are meeting resistance, they have to find another way to try to resolve the problem. The resistance is real, but the answer is not necessarily to blow up the resistance. Instead, they may need to find another way to discover a creative solution.

Develop a "Start-Over" Mentality

During negotiations, parties should consider developing a start-over mentality. A facilitator may give them a situation that is analogous to theirs and ask them to imagine that they are setting up a contract for the first time or that a major competitor has stolen them from their company to operate the competitor's business. Then they are asked, "Would you operate the competitor's business the way your company is being operated now?" This encourages the parties to develop a start-over mentality in which nothing is sacred and they can deal with anything. Analogies help put the parties in other mind-sets so that they can consider what it would be like to start over and generate solutions without the baggage of the past.

Move Around or Take a Break

At times the most effective mechanism for generating creative solutions is to move around or take a break. During the break, the negotiators think about what they would do to solve the problem and then generate two to five ideas to kick-start the process.

Mutual gain negotiations often proceed with approximately a five- minute break every hour. Taking a break gives the parties time to refocus, think, and reflect. Sometimes parties need breaks if the tension gets too high. It is preferable to take a break or reschedule a meeting rather than allow it to deteriorate. The break period helps reduce the emotional intensity, brings the discussion back to the central problem, and restores the negotiations to the mutual gains path.

Brainstorm after the "Sillies"

Creative people are able to generate inventive solutions to problems quite naturally because they regularly think this way. However, creative thinking is not that easy for everyone. Brainstorming is one of the most effective strategies to help people become creative and allow them to think as if they were naturally creative.

Unfortunately, brainstorming has become very structured. This means that linear thinkers have taken away the creative impulse of brainstorming. The methods that rigid brainstormers use force people to produce creative solutions in a certain order. The leader allows each participant in turn to provide a solution. Participants cannot provide ideas out of order. Rigid brainstormers make the process very serious. People do not relax and, consequently, do not break out of assumptions. Instead, they take positions about their solutions. The momentum needed to generate 18th camel solutions is not created.

The challenge is for people to continue to brainstorm after the "sillies"—the period when participants generate ideas that seem so far out or unconventional that they appear to be silly. The first 10 to 15 ideas are usually of high quality. These ideas are most often the ones the negotiators developed prior to the meeting. They may even include the demands that the parties would have presented at the beginning of traditional adversarial negotiations. In mutual gains negotiations, however, those demands and prepared solutions are each listed as one of many possible brainstormed solutions to consider.

The joint brainstorming process does not contribute to the development of the first few ideas. At the beginning of the process, it creates a forum for an "idea dump," which helps the parties see a range of solutions. Just identifying new ideas is not creative, however, because the negotiators are not yet thinking together and spinning off each other's ideas.

After the first 10 to 15 solutions, the quality of the ideas starts to dip. Silly ideas emerge. Most people stop brainstorming at this point because they feel the utility of the process has dropped significantly. It is precisely as a result of those silly ideas, however, that brain cells loosen up, people begin to think creatively, and they move away from assumptions and linear thinking.

The "sillies" are a crucial part of the brainstorming process, and parties should treasure them. They should document, enjoy, and laugh about them. The benefit of the sillies emerges after the parties generate them. The utility curve starts to spike. The sillies loosen up the mind. Suddenly a new idea emerges from the group. Someone piggybacks off that idea, and another idea occurs that is of high quality. The sillies may occur again for a short time, but soon after, the group will again generate a new quality idea.

In one situation that involved the survival of a manufacturing plant, 20 people brainstormed ideas about what could be done. They produced a total of 406 ideas. They filled the walls with 40 flip charts. After prioritizing the ideas, they identified 10 major ones. The group was stunned when they saw that idea number 405 was one of those 10 ideas. The fact that the parties produced this idea so late in the process demonstrated to them that the *entire* brainstorming process was crucial.

Incidentally, 2 of the top 10 ideas came from the 300s and 2 of them from the 200s. Four of the ideas were from the first 40 ideas that the participants brought to the meeting prior to the actual brainstorming process. Brainstorming generated 60 percent of the highest-quality ideas, and independent thought before the process produced 40 percent of the ideas.

An exercise we often employ to illustrate creative brainstorming is to ask groups to think about how they could improve a product—specifically, a bathtub. They reflect about what a "normal" bathtub is: white, hard, and of a specific size. It becomes evident to them that the primary customer is the building contractor. The contractor needs to standardize the size of the bathtub and the location of the plumbing so that these do not become variables in the construction of buildings. The assumption is that customers will find it so inconvenient to change the bathroom that they will be willing to accept the standard bathtub.

When people brainstorm about how to improve the bathtub, they produce ideas such as: "Make it larger, softer, and change the color." Then they consider ideas that are less obvious in areas such as convenience, health, speed, sensuality, and play. In one brainstorming session, the group considered an idea of turning the bathtub into a human car wash. Their idea was that people would move through the bathtub filled with water just as a car moves through a car wash. Brushes would scrub them, sprayers would rinse them, air ducts would blow them dry, and a robot arm would dress them. That silly idea led them to the idea of having a remote device available to fill a bathtub at a selected temperature to be ready just as a person arrived home from a hard day at work. Customer-focused bathtubs come about through brainstorming past the sillies. The humor is wonderful and exciting. Ultimately, the sillies help people expand their thinking and resolve problems that they previously saw as unsolvable.

Companies often use brainstorming in developing new products that are customer focused. For example, Davis and Davidson tell the humorous story of customer-focused toilets in Japan.[17] When the toilet was originally designed, they developed standards that would meet people's needs for usefulness and contractors' requirements for installation without much variability. Apparently, they encountered a new, customer-focused toilet that had heated seats, a musical background, a built-in weighing scale, and the ability to do chemical analyses of waste products and telecommunicate the analysis to the physician of choice for an early warning signal of any health problems. Unfortunately they were not sure how to flush the toilet on this new machine.

Eventually, this product will be commonplace in both hospitals and homes for the elderly as the population continues to age. Ironically, it may also be a source of conflict in the workforce because management will undoubtedly see the opportunity to use such a toilet to test workers for drugs.

Many years ago the telephone ring was also researched. The telephone company wanted to determine what level of irritating ring homeowners would tolerate without being angry with the company, and at the same time, ensuring they would pick up the phone to complete their calls. That generated the telephone ring that we are all familiar with. With similar emphasis on customer service, modern research has resulted in a musical ring of your choice that is appealing to the ear rather than one that forces you to answer the phone.

In most situations, simply identifying a target number of brainstorming ideas forces the negotiating parties to include the sillies and get beyond their normal assumptions. Typically, requiring the negotiators to generate a minimum of 50 to 100 ideas motivates them to produce creative solutions.

Extraordinary results can occur when negotiators brainstorm after the "sillies." Some of the benefits of this method are:

- Anxiety is reduced in the negotiating room because the expression of the ideas helps dispel any myths about them.

- Surprisingly, some of the ideas in the last 20 that are generated are often central to the final decision that will be made. The creativity draws out ideas people never thought of before and helps people reach solutions based on common interests.

- Everyone works together to achieve a common goal of 50 to 100 ideas. The process of collaborating, looking at a flip chart rather than each other, and working together to reach a common goal creates a different climate in the room that helps the group resolve problems more easily.

FACILITATING CREATIVE BRAINSTORMING

Whether the parties decide to work with an external facilitator or to facilitate the process themselves, brainstorming needs facilitation.

The facilitator's job is to make sure that creative brainstorming has the following characteristics:

- It must be nonthreatening.
- The whole process must be nonbinding. Judgments are not allowed. People are encouraged to have fun and laugh throughout the exercise. The sillies are great opportunities to enhance the relationship between the negotiators.
- An abundance of ideas are stimulated.

On occasion, the parties may have some difficulty generating many ideas. Facilitators may encourage participants to suggest ideas in many ways such as:

- Remind everyone that the brainstormed ideas are nonbinding. Any idea generated during brainstorming is written on flip charts with "nonbinding" at the top. All the flip charts will eventually be ripped up.
- After each idea is suggested, encourage participants to give more ideas.
- Be sure to continue brainstorming after the sillies and to give the participants recognition for the sillies because they are valid assumption breakers.
- Repeat each idea out loud so that everyone hears it. This is useful because people make a lot of noise while they brainstorm, and they will focus on you as the hub to help them stimulate additional ideas. It also allows you time to write down each word exactly as it is said.
- Support "piggybacking," which is the spinoff of one idea from another. Write down piggyback ideas as separate ideas.

- When people run out of ideas, it is important to get "every drop of water out of the wet towel." To squeeze it dry and secure the last few ideas, ask each participant what he or she thinks. When someone has an idea, see if the idea generates more thought from other people. Sometimes you can get participants to generate as many as 10 to 15 more ideas by pushing them a little further.
- Take a break. Sometimes it's best to take a break and tell participants to return with one idea each. This will help identify any more ideas that may be left.

The Flip-Charting Technique

The term "flip-charting technique" may sound mundane, but people often underestimate the power of this skill to stimulate creative brainstorming. Negotiators who facilitate the creative brainstorming themselves need to have this skill. Some of the core techniques in flip-charting are:

• **Write down everything exactly as it is said.** Perhaps the worst error in flip-charting is for the person with the pen to write his or her own words instead of the participant's words. The person who is writing on the flip chart must be a scribe, not an editor. A person who communicates an idea has a right to have it written exactly as it was said. The scribe should repeat the idea out loud. This ensures that he or she says exactly what the person said. The scribe should not write the idea in a shorthand fashion but precisely as the participant said it.

• **Write down ideas even if you do not understand them or do not agree with them.** It is not important for the facilitator to understand the idea or agree with it at this point. The ideas must be written down as they are said without being challenged. You lose momentum if you start questioning the ideas as the participants state them. Just record the ideas.

• **Number each item.** This is extremely important for the next step. Numbering each idea helps the participants refer to the items and converge them into categories in order to find a complete solution.

• **Write down the sillies.** Many people argue that the sillies should be ignored. On the contrary, what might be silly to you may be very serious to the person who stated the idea, and since you should not judge the comments made, write them down the way you hear them. Furthermore, a silly idea generates laughter the first time a person states it. As you write the silly idea and repeat it out loud at the same time, it generates laughter again. Finally, when you review the item, it generates laughter a third time. If you can get three laughs from a group that is in conflict, you should not pass up the opportunity.

• **Rotate people to record ideas on the flip charts.** Everybody within the group should have the opportunity to be the facilitator and do the flip-charting. Negotiations take a long time, and the facilitation role needs to be dispersed among the negotiators. Even if the parties use external facilitation, each negotiator can facilitate one flip-chart page and record 8 to 10 ideas. This allows everyone to be involved and to share in the facilitation process. Emphasize that spelling does not matter. Display the completed flip charts on the wall so all can see them. This allows everyone to review all the ideas that have been suggested. It also gives the negotiators a sense of accomplishment when they see the number of ideas they have generated.

• **Use computer technology for brainstorming.** Technology is available that allows a computer to be used for recording ideas during nonbinding creative brainstorming. The ideas are entered into the computer and are shown on a screen as people state them. This process has some strengths and weaknesses. The strengths are:

– The sorting exercise after the brainstorming is more efficient because you can move the ideas around more easily on the computer.

– The computer type is more professional and the process allows you to generate ideas quickly on screen in large print so everyone can see them.

– Handwriting and spelling problems that occur on flip charts are avoided using the computer.

Some of the weaknesses of using a computer system for nonbinding creative brainstorming include:

- People get the impression that the brainstormed ideas will be saved. They know that flip charts will be destroyed because they can be ripped up in front of the participants. Once the ideas are in the computer, all of them may be saved and may threaten the nonbinding nature of the exercise.

- Only those who have the skill to enter the information in the computer can record the brainstormed ideas. As a result, all the participants cannot be involved in the facilitation process and will miss another opportunity to develop relationships.

If the trust is there to use the technology and the parties have the ability and desire to experiment with it, it can be very useful to expedite the negotiations.

What Is the Outcome of Nonbinding Creative Brainstorming?

The outcome of nonbinding creative brainstorming is a very long list of ideas. Some of the ideas will be consistent with the common interests and some will not. However, participants often are delighted about the following:

- The abundance of ideas that are generated.
- Almost anything possible is said.
- There are no hidden agendas. All the ideas are on the flip charts.
- Often, some ideas on the flip charts will be useful when the parties develop a solution based upon the common interests.

GENERATE POTENTIAL SOLUTIONS

The great writer Stephen Leacock was reputed to have said about writing a speech that you should jot down ideas as they occur to you and that while the "jotting" is simple, the "occurring" is difficult. The parties identify potential solutions during the problem-resolution process. The expectation is that because the parties know and understand the problem and have engaged in nonbinding creative brainstorming, they will have a significantly enhanced ability to converge ideas and identify several mutual gains solutions.

After brainstorming any problem, the participants fill the walls with flip charts containing many ideas about how to resolve the problem. Imagine staring at the flip charts and the multitude of ideas. You may recognize that you do not know what to do with all this information. How can you separate the chaff from the wheat? You need a process to narrow the number of ideas and to converge to potential mutual gains solutions.

While the brainstorming process includes humor and laughter, the converging process is much more serious and staid. In this step, the participants propose solutions that answer the problem and then begin to discuss and assess which potential solution best meets the common interests.

The negotiators will need facilitation (whether it is one of the negotiators or an external facilitator) to converge and assess the brainstormed ideas. This section focuses on the facilitation techniques needed to do the convergence and assessment process. It is presented in four steps:

Step 1—Cluster Brainstormed Ideas by Themes

Step 2—Generate Several Solutions from the Themes

Step 3—Engage in a Risk/Benefit Analysis

Step 4—Choose a Preferred Solution

Step 1—Cluster Brainstormed Ideas by Themes

After groups complete nonbinding brainstorming, they begin the convergence process. Although the negotiators are getting closer to solutions, the clustering process is still nonbinding. Ideas that are included in the theme clusters can be removed later.

Clustering ideas into themes can be done with everyone present or with just the leaders of each of the groups (usually one or two people representing each of the parties). They review each of the brainstormed ideas on the flip charts. A facilitator helps with the exercise in the following manner:

- Reviews the list of common interests to refresh the parties' memories.

- Reviews the list of brainstormed ideas. Clarifies the ones that are unclear and makes nonbinding minor edits to those ideas that may be more acceptable to both parties and consistent with at least one common interest, if slightly modified.

- Circles the brainstormed ideas that are worthy of further exploration and are consistent with at least one of the common interests. By circling an idea, the parties are not agreeing to accept it. The circle only means that the idea has some potential to contribute to a common interest solution. Typically, about a third of the brainstormed ideas are circled and can contribute (in whole or in part) to the development of common-interest solutions.

The entire group then clusters the different solutions around the themes. The process works as follows:

- All the circled ideas that potentially reflect the common interests are read off.

- The proposed themes are identified and agreed to by the participants.

- The themes are written on separate blank flip charts.
- The circled ideas and numbers are called out. The facilitator writes down the numbers of the ideas under the appropriate themes, and the participants cross the numbers off the brainstormed list. The new flip charts are titled by theme and contain lists of ideas identified by numbers.
- The themes are divided among the participants and they write the ideas associated with each of the numbers. For example, if "job security" or "organization change" is a major theme, a flip chart is devoted to that topic. All the ideas associated with the numbers under that topic are recorded and rewritten on that flip chart. If the parties use a computer system for this exercise, these ideas can be entered into the system. People can see the list on the screen and can also have hard copies to work with during this exercise.
- The flip charts containing all the original creative ideas generated earlier are removed. They are not disposed of yet because they may be useful if a solution based on the circled ideas and consistent with the common interests has not been generated.

At the end of this process, the participants have flip charts that list all the ideas consistent with the common interests. On the basis of these ideas they will attempt to reach a common interest-based solution.

Examples of Theme Clusters in Mutual Gains Negotiations

During mutual gains negotiations, parties have identified many theme clusters. Some examples of common-interest themes that have been acceptable to unions and companies include the following:

- Compensation and benefits.
- New technology.
- Training.
- Communications.
- Rewards and incentives.
- Leadership style.
- Reorganization.
- Simplifying the collective agreement.
- Working conditions.
- Health and safety.
- Personnel changes.
- Hours of work.
- Changing the way things are done.
- Discipline strategies.
- Customer relations.
- Improving morale.
- Supplier relationships.
- Procedures.
- Standardized approaches.
- Productivity improvements.
- Cross-functional work.
- Additional data requirements.

The above list is a small representation of the kinds of themes that appear in this process. You may notice the breadth of themes that emerge. Obviously, the list reflects the kinds of topics that parties address in mutual gains negotiations.

Step 2—Generate Several Solutions from the Themes

Here's where the magic begins. Both parties are now looking at a wall with flip charts displaying the following:

- The problem.
- The stakeholders.
- The facts that are known and to be known.
- Each party's individual interests.
- The common interests.
- The creative ideas listed under themes and potentially consistent with the common interests.

The participants review all the flip charts. They begin to see several alternative solutions and directions that the solutions can take based on the common interests.

The participants generate several alternative solutions. Typically, the parties should address a minimum of three common-interest solutions. These solutions are nonbinding. This means that you are not proposing a solution you suggest as your solution to the problem. Even at this point of the dispute-resolution process, it is important to generate new possibilities.

Developing alternative solutions requires some thought and reflection. To be true to the process, the participants need to ensure that the potential solutions are consistent with the ideas that are on the theme flip charts reflecting the common interests.

Step 3—Engage in a Risk/Benefit Analysis

In this step the negotiators assess the risks and benefits of the solutions. They ask the following questions:

- Is it a wise solution?
- Is the solution simple enough for everyone to understand?
- Does the solution enhance the relationship so that the parties will be able to resolve a dispute effectively the next time?

This analysis may cause negotiators to modify the potential solution so that it is wiser or simpler. The process usually involves some serious face-to-face discussions and negotiations about the best solution to select.

The negotiators then review the list of stakeholders and consider which ones will win or lose as a result of the alternative solutions. They ask themselves:

- Are there any stakeholders who are at risk in this solution?

- Who are the winners?

- Who are the losers?

- Who are the "accidental losers"—those people or groups who do not seem to have anything to do with the problem but who may take a loss as a result of a potential solution. In a case described earlier, for example, labor and management did not identify their accidental losers. They made a decision that was in their mutual interest—to move to a shorter workweek. Unfortunately, the accidental loser was the customer who needed service five days a week. Because the parties did not consider the customer, business was lost and all players became losers.

   There should never be any unknown accidental losers. If you identify accidental losers and you cannot prevent them from losing, find a way to reduce the damage to them. If that is not possible, at least develop a communication strategy that anticipates the probable negative responses by those stakeholders.

   Participants in a dispute can discover accidental losers by engaging in a "ripple effect" analysis in which they ask what will be the effect when a solution is in place. Then, they consider what the effect may cause. By examining the ripple effects of the solution, the participants may discover some accidental losers who had nothing to do with the problem and who may be at risk.

Step 4—Choose a Preferred Solution

Negotiators then assess each of the alternative potential solutions that have emerged from this process. The total quality movement has generated some useful weighing techniques to help determine which solution has the best potential of resolving the problem. Those techniques work well if the negotiating parties accept all the solutions equally. If that is not the case, then direct discussions and negotiations will take place concerning which solution to accept.

The step of choosing the preferred solution is done collaboratively or independently, depending on the trust level between the parties, the complexity of the problem, and the quality of the potential solutions.

Joint Selection of the Preferred Solution

When trust is reasonably high and the potential solutions not very contentious, the parties can try to choose a preferred solution together. In most situations, if they are considering three alternative solutions, the risk/benefit analysis will generate a fourth solution that combines the best parts of the other three. After this fourth solution is generated, the parties consider their common and separate interests and adjust the solution as necessary to reach agreement. At this point, the parties can dispose of all the flip charts because they are now unnecessary for any future use.

Independent Selection of the Preferred Solution

In lower-trust negotiations and when the potential solutions are more contentious, the parties can meet separately to review the potential solutions. They may decide which potential solution or variation of a potential solution best meets their interests and the common interests. After determining their proposed solutions, they bring them back to the negotiating table for direct discussions. The parties negotiate their solutions and attempt to reach an agreement. After agreement, they destroy the flip charts containing the brainstormed ideas.

What if They Do Not Agree on a Common-Interest Solution?

Sometimes parties cannot reach solutions through the common-interest ideas. If that is the case, the participants return to their original list of brainstormed ideas. The process is similar to the one above with the following modifications:

- On the original nonbinding list of brainstormed ideas, the participants identify those that were not circled and separate the remaining ideas into three groups:
  1. Ideas in support of the union's interests.
  2. Ideas in support of the company's interests.
  3. Ideas that no one supports.
- The parties prepare two lists—one for ideas in support of the union's interests and the other for those in support of the company's interests. The participants now have flip charts that record common-interest solutions grouped under themes and solutions from each of the parties that reflect their individual interests.
- Then the participants destroy all of the brainstormed ideas. They have no usefulness anymore because all the ideas of value have been recorded on other flip charts (or entered into the computer, if the parties are using that technology).
- Next, the parties attempt to generate alternative solutions that include the common-interest ideas and that meet some of the essential separate interests. Once again, the negotiating parties generate three to five alternative solutions.
- The process from this point on is precisely the same as described above in Steps 3 and 4. To determine if the solutions are wise and simple, the negotiating parties

engage in a risk/benefit analysis on the new potential solutions. They also identify the winners and losers and any accidental losers.

- They then proceed together or independently to do a final analysis of the solutions and identify the preferred solution. Through discussion and negotiation, they reach agreement on the solution.

A CASE EXAMPLE: APPLYING MUTUAL GAINS TO COMMUNICATIONS AND CONFIDENTIALITY

In negotiations, trust between parties can be sacrificed quickly in the areas of communications and confidentiality, yet parties often neglect to address these very important issues. Many problems can result if parties do not discuss the issues of communications and confidentiality. For example:

- **In the absence of information, people make up information.** In negotiations, a clear communication method and timeline should be established to slow down the rumor mill. People are not satisfied when they do not know what is happening. They prefer to have any information, even if it is false. They prefer rumors to not knowing.

Additionally, employees will believe the first information they receive if it is from a credible source. One union used this knowledge to their advantage and prided themselves on being able to communicate faster than management to employees. The union network was lightning fast, while management filtered information before it was disseminated.

- **When confidentiality is disregarded, trust is broken.** Lack of confidentiality is a major trust breaker in negotiations, especially when parties are trying to build trust in mutual gains negotiations. One break of confidentiality could sabotage the entire relationship.

A serious break of confidentiality occurred when a company decided to expose specific financial information to the union negotiators. It was understood that the union would keep this information confidential. The union distributed the information to all the employees and to the newspapers, who printed it the next day. Management felt betrayed by the lack of confidentiality, but because the relationship was strong, the parties were able to discuss the issue openly and rebuild the relationship. After this situation, however, management presented information in a more guarded fashion, sometimes withholding information because it was not yet in the public domain.

If parties want to use communication and confidentiality as a trust builder rather than as a trust destroyer, then they should agree on these issues during the getting-started phase of the negotiations. The agreement should address what information will be confidential and what will be public.

In a recent negotiation, we applied the problem-solving approach to the issues of communications and confidentiality and developed important results that guided the parties throughout the negotiations. The value of presenting the results of this process are twofold:

1. First, the results may help other negotiators set up guidelines for their negotiations on communications and confidentiality during the getting-started phase.

2. Second, they illustrate how a problem may look when it is resolved (as described in Chapters 6 and this chapter), and they identify the information that may be saved as a matter of record after parties reach agreement on an issue.

The parties negotiated according to the approach described in this book. The results are presented as follows:

- Joint problem.
- Interests.
- Facts.
- Summary of the brainstormed ideas.
- Agreement reached on this issue.

The following summarizes the results of their work:

What Is the Joint Problem Statement?

How are we going to release information in a timely, accurate, and confidential manner during negotiations and during ratification to maximize understanding?

What Are the Interests in This Case?

The union's interests include:

- How to ensure that everyone has the same understanding of the information.
- When to release information.
- How to keep the membership informed.
- How to deal with the pressure to communicate.
- How to communicate within their own group.
- How the communication will take place.
- How management communicates to the rest of management.
- How managers may influence union representatives before they vote on ratification.
- How to ensure that information is not released too early so that when the union has a meeting to ratify they get a large turnout.

The company's interests include:

- When to release information.
- The concern that information will be released before it is final and will potentially contradict the final agreement.
- How the communication will take place.
- Confidentiality.

Common interests include:

- When to release information.

- Concern that information will be released before it is final and people will operate on inaccurate information.
- Confidentiality.
- How the communication will take place.
- A method of ensuring that everyone has the same understanding of the information.
- Pressure to keep the constituencies informed.
- Managers' influence on the unionized employees during the process of ratification.

What Are the Facts in This Case?

- Nothing is certain until agreement.
- During the last negotiations, problems occurred when information was released. Managers negatively influenced people during ratification.
- Some managers do not keep information confidential when you tell them about the contract.
- All managers and employees should have the same kind of information.
- Even with perfect agreement, we will get complainers.
- The unofficial communication of information often occurs before the final contract.
- There are rumor mills.
- The union will release the information after the signed memorandum at one time.
- Another company has a 1-800 number for updates on negotiations that is available to anybody. It tells what issues are being discussed, but it does not provide results.
- The different constituencies of the union and management often complain that they are not getting enough information.

- The managers complain that they get information from the union rather than hearing it directly from management.

Nonbinding Brainstormed Ideas (after clustering ideas under categories)

This section is presented for information purposes, although this shortened list of brainstormed ideas would normally *not* be saved after negotiations.

- How will communications be managed?
  - Tell the constituencies what information they will be getting.
  - Explain why they will be receiving the amount of information they will get.
  - Explain that they are going to know when the deal is set.
- How much detail will be communicated?
  - It will be decided by the bargaining teams.
  - It will be sufficient to make the agreement clear to all.
  - None, until the parties finally settle the deal (this is during the ratification).
- What will be the timing and scheduling of communications?
  - The bargaining teams will decide this during the negotiations.
  - At the time of ratification, communication will occur.
- Who will present the information when it is released?
  - The bargaining committee.
  - Human resources.
  - The union only.
  - The managers communicating directly to the employees.

- Who will receive the information?
  - During bargaining, managers and employees should receive negotiation updates at the same time.
  - After bargaining, negotiators will release the information to both the union and managers at the same time.
- What will be the vehicles of communication?
  - E-mail.
  - A 1-800 number, which will be a joint number.
  - Paper communications.
  - Seminars, voice mail, and phone calls.
- Training, development, and education.
  - A road show will be conducted after ratification.
  - After the deal, every manager with unionized employees will get information.
  - They will also get a synopsis of the method used in mutual gains negotiating.
  - Managers may become informed sufficiently to deliver training about the contract.

The Agreed Upon Solution to This Problem

Prenegotiations:

- An issue statement will be sent out to all managers and employees about how communications will proceed during negotiations and at ratification time.
- After giving an agenda to the company, the union will release it to its membership. The company will release the union's agenda as well as its proposals after they are tabled in negotiations.

During negotiations:

- The joint bargaining committees will prepare updates to be released to all managers and employees at the same time.

- The information may be over multiple communication vehicles, depending on which is the most appropriate.
- Joint and separate releases may occur during negotiations.
- Updates will not give details of information but indicate that the parties are still talking.

At ratification time:

- The union will be given a fair opportunity to talk in an untainted way to their membership.

After ratification:

- A road show to managers will be conducted describing how the negotiations proceeded and what is in the contract.

A COMMENT FOR SOPHISTICATED NEGOTIATORS

Following the process is key to success for a negotiator, but it should never become a burden to problem resolution. The process should add value rather than being a barrier to reaching agreement.

Some problems have obvious solutions to which all parties can agree immediately. One negotiator referred to a solution like this as a "BFO" or a "blinding flash of the obvious." It would be a waste of time and emotional energy to use the entire process on this kind of issue. The parties should just agree and move on to the next problem.

Other problems may not have such obvious solutions, so the negotiator has to follow the process closely. It may be useful to know what each side wants up front simply to understand the magnitude of the differences. Sometimes this can help focus the discussions about interests and facts.

The process is the foundation to which a negotiator returns regularly to reach agreements. Novice negotiators would be wise to stay much closer to the mutual gains process, for they may not know how to return to the path once they deviate and get lost. The experienced mutual gains negotiator knows when to diverge from the process and when to return gracefully. Just as a conductor knows when to get more drama from the wind instruments or gentleness from the violins, a skilled negotiator senses when to diverge from the process in order to find the path of least resistance to a mutual gains agreement.

SUMMARY

- The mutual gains process of negotiating generates new and inventive solutions that enhance the ability of parties to resolve problems and achieve union-management peace.

- In mutual gains negotiations, parties make every attempt to resolve problems directly rather than trade wins and losses.

- The real benefit of mutual gains negotiations is the joint discovery process. Parties generate nonbinding creative ideas and discover creative solutions. Through this process, they find wise, simple, and relationship-enhancing solutions.

- Brainstorming should be nonbinding.

- When people are in conflict with others, the assumptions that have helped them the most in other situations often lead them to resist new ideas and obstruct problem resolution.

- Most people solve problems through linear thinking.

- Creative people often look for solutions to problems by thinking from a different perspective. Rather than moving forward, they may start at the end and go backwards.

- The principle in brainstorming is to find the path of least resistance.

- Sometimes a solution to a problem is easier to discover if the parties can recognize the extremes of the solution.
- During negotiations, parties should consider developing a start-over mentality.
- At times the most effective mechanism for generating creative solutions is to move around or take a break.
- Brainstorming is one of the most effective strategies to help people become creative and allow them to think as if they were naturally creative.
- The challenge is for people to continue to brainstorm after the "sillies"—the period when participants generate ideas that seem so far out or unconventional that they appear to be silly.
- The "sillies" are a crucial part of the brainstorming process, and parties should treasure them. They should document, enjoy, and laugh about them.
- Extraordinary results can occur when negotiators brainstorm after the "sillies."
- Some of the core techniques in flip-charting are:
  - Write down everything exactly as it is said.
  - Write down ideas even if you do not understand them or do not agree with them.
  - Number each item.
  - Write down the sillies.
  - Rotate people to record ideas on the flip charts.
  - Use computer technology for brainstorming.
- The facilitation techniques needed to converge and assess ideas are:
  - Step 1—Cluster Brainstormed Ideas by Themes
  - Step 2—Generate Several Solutions from the Themes
  - Step 3—Engage in a Risk/Benefit Analysis
  - Step 4—Choose a Preferred Solution

- In negotiations, trust between parties can be sacrificed quickly in the areas of communications and confidentiality, yet parties often neglect to address these very important issues.

- A key success factor for a negotiator is to follow the process but to never let it become a burden to problem resolution.

- The experienced mutual gains negotiator knows when to diverge from the process and when to return gracefully. Novice negotiators would be wise to stay much closer to the mutual gains process, for they may not know how to return to the path once they deviate and get lost.

CHAPTER 8

How to Reach an Agreement

A centipede went to the Wise Old Owl and said, "I've got a serious case of arthritis. What should I do?" The Owl pondered and replied, "I have the answer—turn yourself into a flamingo! You could stand on one leg and rest the other, then reverse the process!" The ecstatic centipede exclaimed, "You are a genius! The Owl of Brilliance! I have only one more question, if I may?" "Certainly," said the Owl. "What is the question?" The centipede replied, "How do I change into a flamingo?" "Sorry, I'm Policy, not Operations," responded the Owl.

Mutual gains solutions do not emerge from theoretical procedures and processes. The best idea has great difficulty becoming a reality. A mutual gains negotiations process often provides benefits for each party, but it is not necessarily an easy way to reach agreement. The solution needs to have limited "waste," which means that the agreement should have simple solutions that meet most of the underlying interests of all parties and can be done.

The previous three phases of negotiating—planning, starting face-to-face negotiations, and mutual gains problem solving—must be completed. The fourth phase, reaching mutual gains collective agreements, makes the process applicable.

DO NOT LET DESPERATION BE YOUR INSPIRATION

The following are some useful guidelines that help negotiators through this vital phase of reaching agreement in mutual gains contract negotiations:

• **Do not lose your perspective.** Negotiators need to focus on the mutual gains agreement and not lose perspective. When the end is in sight, parties may feel desperate and rush to an agreement before they are ready. Common errors resulting from desperation include getting too pushy and regressing to adversarial techniques, opening up issues the parties can do nothing about, and becoming indiscreet about confidentiality and communications.

• **An agreement that is good enough today is good enough tomorrow.** It is worth spending the extra day to make sure the collective agreement says what you really want it to say. If the solution is truly of mutual gain, then solutions that are good enough today will also be good enough tomorrow. The parties can spend a day checking how effective and accurate their solutions are.

• **A good deal sells itself.** When an agreement is a good deal, negotiators do not have to push. The deal should sell itself. Parties should allow time for their counterparts to do their own internal selling. Parties may confuse their counterparts by pushing a mutual gains agreement. They may also make it harder to close the agreement. If the other party doesn't accept a good deal, parties can try a one-line comment such as, "You are not going to let a deal go by for 25 cents, are you?" This should get the other side thinking about whether they are being too stubborn or whether they are really taking a stand on a principle.

• **Nothing is binding until agreement.** It is common practice in mutual gains negotiations that parties do not agree to anything until the entire agreement is reached. The agreement will have a total balance sheet that demonstrates mutual gains. Most solutions will be based on the common or separate interests, but some solutions are trade-offs. Even in mutual gains negotiations, some give-and-take exists.

COMPLETING CONTRACT NEGOTIATIONS

Some negotiators are able to achieve mutual gains solutions but have difficulty reaching an overall agreement using this approach. The following describes what should be done to complete mutual gains contract negotiations successfully.

Ongoing Writing of Language

Traditionally, parties write the language after they sign a memorandum and reach an agreement. Typically, management writes the language, often under great time pressure. It is not surprising that occasionally the language does not accurately reflect what was really negotiated. One simple word such as "must" changed to "should" makes a very big difference.

Modern technology allows parties to see the language of an article on a screen as they negotiate. The article can be written as the negotiators recommend solutions. The parties can explore alternative language and study the implications of different words.

In some situations, the parties may agree to some of the word changes in an article but leave blanks for the sections they still need to discuss. They may leave blanks for words such as "should," "must," and "ought to" until they complete their discussion of the actual meaning of the words. In other cases, the parties might write the entire article during the negotiations rather than waiting to write it after they complete the negotiations.

When computer technology is not available, the parties can write the articles and modify them on flip charts during the negotiations. By jointly writing the articles, they reduce the possibility of falling out of trust after negotiations, when the company might prepare language inconsistent with what was actually negotiated. A company may do this inadvertently, but the union may feel it is intentional. If this occurs, the company loses its credibility.

When a company writes the contract after the negotiations, we recommend that at least one union negotiator attend the writing sessions so that the company will reflect the intent of the agreement in the contract. It is acting in bad faith for a party to try to gain against its counterpart by adjusting the writing so that it does not reflect the parties' agreement. It is very difficult to recover from a "gotcha" deal like this.

Analyses Done Separately before Signing the Agreement

Some steps are crucial before signing a collective labor agreement. Separately, the parties take these steps before signing an agreement:

- **Do a complete costing of the collective agreement.**
  Costing should be an ongoing activity as each problem
  is negotiated. As the negotiations draw to a close, the
  parties undertake a final costing to determine the total
  worth of the new contract and how it differs from the
  past agreement.
- **Develop a list of "killer questions" from the perspective of the key stakeholders who will review the
  agreement.** Parties develop a full list of questions and
  then devise responses they can use in communi-cations
  after they sign the agreement. Unions and management
  have occasionally done this jointly.
- **Decide whether the mutual gains agreement is equal
  to or better than what parties would have negotiated
  through the rights or power approaches.** The parallel
  planning committee (if any) is often involved in this
  review.
- **Presell the agreement to key influencers to increase
  the likelihood that key constituencies understand
  and accept it.** Ensure that the extent and method of

communications are consistent with the confidentiality and communications agreement the negotiating parties developed at the outset of negotiations.

Review Recommended Agreement with Key Stakeholders

In almost every case, the parties need to consult the key stakeholders before they reach an agreement. In the union, the national representatives are often the stakeholders who need input, while within the company, the senior executive often becomes involved.

The parties need to present the recommended agreement to the key stakeholders in a way that helps them understand how they reached their conclusions. Mutual gains solutions are commonly far more creative than traditional solutions. This may surprise some key stakeholders.

Keeping stakeholders apprised of developments may be useful so that they are able to work with the negotiators at the final stages of negotiations. Senior executives or national union representatives often step in toward the end of problematic negotiations and undermine the work of the negotiators. Frequently, this occurs because they do not understand how the negotiators reached their conclusions and they get nervous. Managing the anxiety of people who are not doing the negotiating is important in resolving issues whether the parties use the mutual gains approach or traditional bargaining.

Reach an Agreement

At this point, the parties are ready to shake hands, but they haven't finished the deal. Senior management has to give final approval, and the membership has to ratify the agreement. After this, the toughest task lies ahead—living by the agreement.

In mutual gains negotiating, when the parties are at the point of reaching agreement, they discuss the mechanisms that support the new contract. Some of these might include union management councils, methods to support continuous negotiations, and dispute resolution.

If the collective agreement reflects the values and principles the parties adhered to in the negotiations, the parties need to consider how to ensure that their people incorporate those values in their daily work. Some strategies companies and unions have used successfully in this regard are:

- **Ensure that the principles and values demonstrated in the negotiations process become part of the collective labor agreement.** In this way, the agreement will outlive the career of the negotiators and become a right that union and management have to live by. When the agreement is verbal, the level of slippage is high when a senior manager leaves a company or a union leader is removed from the bargaining situation.

- **Develop joint union-management teams within the company that will deal with ongoing union-management problem solving.** Joint union-management teams can resolve problems before they grow out of proportion, and many organizations have had success with these teams. One company introduced joint steward-foreman counseling for the first step of a grievance process. The discussion was only about the problem, the facts, the stakeholders, and the interests. But because people were embarrassed to speak in front of a steward about their complaint if they didn't have one, spurious complaints disappeared from the list of grievances.

- **Engage in joint union-management training in the area of joint problem solving.** In one situation, representatives of both the company and the union were trained to lead joint problem-solving training. They then led the training as cotrainers. The impact was dramatic because they modeled the kind of relationship the company wanted to see their employees demonstrate on a daily basis.

Companies and unions have used the new contract, which includes values and intent as well as principles, to introduce a new way of working within the company. Often, the rest of the company is skeptical about what occurs in mutual gains negotiations. They need to be exposed to what is occurring. They also need to bring greater democracy into the workplace, to empower people, and to enhance the appreciation of diversity of all people to maximize the gains for the company, the union, and the employees. The ultimate success of all those parties will be in the hands of the customer. It is the customer who continues to support the business and assists in ensuring that everybody's needs are met and that the enterprise flourishes.

Sign the Memorandum of Agreement

The memorandum may look just like the one the parties signed when they engaged in traditional bargaining. This ultimately is what the membership and the senior executive see as a result of the bargaining process.

By signing the agreement the negotiators demonstrate their 100 percent commitment to what they negotiated. Once they sign it, they own the entire agreement even if they have difficulty with parts of it. They cannot claim that they did not agree with part of it. When the two parties sign the agreement, they consent to everything in it and are jointly recommending it as a common solution. A deal is a deal. Parties fall out of trust very quickly if they backtrack after they sign an agreement.

Present the Agreement for Approval

After the union signs the agreement, they bring it to the membership for a vote. Hopefully, the vote will be in favor of the agreement. On occasion, unions vote down agreements that were secured in mutual gains negotiations. Because of the creative process, an agreement can sometimes be different from normal agreements and the membership does not understand it sufficiently. As a result, the negotiators must be diligent in communicating what the agreement is, what it means, and what it is not. Before constituents vote, they need to understand the agreement. If they are confused about any part of it, they may vote against it.

On the company side, the senior executive waits for the union to approve the agreement. If the company has a parallel planning committee operating, they are on red alert awaiting the vote count or, in some situations, a deadline in the negotiations process. If the vote is negative or the deadline is not met, they mobilize to try to reduce the damage to the company caused by a strike.

The union has a similar team that determines what to do in the event of a strike. They have a strike fund and make plans about where to strike if it should occur.

It is very important that the strike and lockout teams operate independently from the negotiating teams when they identify how they would resort to power if that is required. Parties should resort to power only as a better alternative to the negotiated agreement. The union and company must have separate teams working on their individual strategies in order to maintain integrity for the negotiating members. Everyone knows that there are power teams operating in the company and the union. The objective of the union and management negotiators is to avoid having to resort to power and to negotiate a solution that meets or exceeds any agreement the power approach would yield.

Ratify the Agreement

With the approvals in place, the parties can ratify the agreement. They now have the document in place and all the signatures. The negotiators can now call home and say that they will be returning very soon.

Celebrate

It's time for the negotiators to congratulate themselves for a job well done. In more enlightened union-management environments, the negotiators celebrate together, but celebrating separately is also totally appropriate. The union congratulates themselves because they feel that they earned a victory and met their membership's needs while maintaining the company's survival and meeting the customers' needs. The company celebrates because they have met the needs of their shareholders, the union, and the employees, while enhancing the satisfaction of their customers. Everyone is a winner. It's time to go home.

Publish the Agreement

With the celebration complete, many people forget to publish the agreement quickly. At this point, only the negotiators really know how well they did. The managers and the employees do not fully understand what the new order of work will be and how they will collaborate in the future. It is important to publish the agreement as soon as possible so that everyone will know what occurred and an environment can be created for union-management peace.

Conduct a Process Review after Negotiations

All negotiators should be present to do a process review at the conclusion of negotiations. This will also be an opportunity for joint celebration on the success of the initiative. The process review should consider the following:

- What are the strengths and weaknesses of the previous negotiations?
- What should be done to sustain and enhance the momentum generated from these negotiations throughout the term of the contract?
- What should be done differently and what should be done in the same manner during the next collective bargaining?

The results of the process review should be given to each of the negotiating team members. It is often appropriate for the person who conducted the initial training to facilitate the process review. He or she may be able to close the loop and provide feedback on how effective the negotiators were at implementing what they learned at the beginning of this process.

Communicate and Educate All Employees about the New Agreement

Many organizations neglect this step. At a minimum, the company should engage employees in a learning process about the collective agreement—what changes will occur as a result and what it means for the management group. Union leadership should take the opportunity to communicate a similar message to its constituencies.

In more enlightened organizations, the company and union do the training jointly with representatives from both groups in the audience. Through the joint training process, the parties demonstrate the new environment created throughout the negotiations.

At this point, parties may train everyone in joint problem solving so that they can live by this agreement on a regular basis. Also, the parties may teach them how to resolve problems at the source rather than going through a grievance route.

EVALUATE THE NEGOTIATIONS

Evaluation is an essential component of any negotiation. The most obvious evaluation for the union will be the vote by their membership. If they pass the recommended collective agreement, then the membership's evaluation is that the contract is acceptable. For the management negotiators, approval of senior management and ratification by union membership provides an evaluation of an acceptable contract.

In addition to the above scorecard, mutual gains negotiators often ask themselves how well they did on specific problems and in the overall negotiations. Some of the self-evaluation methods they use include:

- Identifying whether the solutions are wise, simple, and enhance the relationship.
- Determining which of the stakeholders will be the winners, losers, and accidental losers.
- Using a grading system.

The first two methods were discussed earlier in the book. The third method is a technique that can be very useful during and after negotiations. It is a grading system to evaluate the solutions for each negotiated problem as well as the results of the overall collective agreement.

There are four grade levels in mutual gains negotiations. In some negotiations, the four possible grades are printed on a flip chart and posted on the wall (Figure 8–1).

FIGURE   8 – 1

The Four Grades of an Agreement

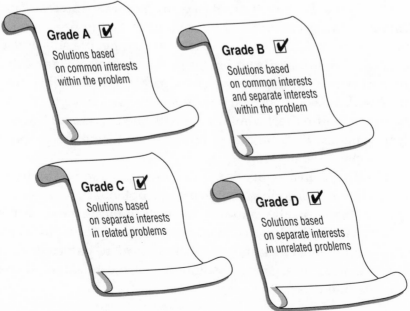

Grade A ☑
Solutions based on common interests within the problem

Grade B ☑
Solutions based on common interests and separate interests within the problem

Grade C ☑
Solutions based on separate interests in related problems

Grade D ☑
Solutions based on separate interests in unrelated problems

To pass the mutual gains negotiations "course" with high marks, the parties need to reach the highest grades—A or B. Adversarial negotiations rarely exceed grades C or D. However, even a D is a passing grade (although just barely) because an agreement is concluded.

The negotiators may evaluate solutions during negotiation of each problem by assigning a grade level to each one. Additionally, the negotiators can determine the overall grade of the entire agreement at a negotiation debriefing meeting. They can do this separately or jointly after the negotiations.

The following describes each of the grades in detail.

• **Grade A—Solutions Based on Common Interests within the Problem.** People can easily communicate solutions based on common interests within the problem because people understand the solution. They recognize that the solution is a mutual gains conclusion, and in most cases, they can live by it with greater ease. The techniques of generating potential solutions explain how parties can develop these kinds of solutions. The grievance problem described at the outset of Chapter 7 is an example of this level of solution.

• **Grade B—Solutions Based on Separate Interests and Common Interests within the Problem.** A Grade B solution is more complex than a Grade A solution, but people still understand that the solution is within the problem. They recognize that the parties met common as well as separate interests when they generated the solution. The constituencies who have to live by the decision often feel comfortable with the agreement because they recognize that the negotiators worked inside the problem and reached a solution.

Mutual gains negotiations often include Grade B solutions. The techniques described for generating potential solutions that are not based on the common interests indicate how parties identify Grade B solutions. In Chapter 6, the situation in which union and management negotiate about how to pay facilitators is an example of a Grade B solution that meets common and separate interests.

• **Grade C—Solutions Based on Separate Interests in Related Problems.** This grade of solution is far more complex than the previous two and much more difficult to understand from an external perspective. External constituencies who have to live by these solutions perceive that the negotiators made a trade-off between one problem and another. Typically, in traditional bargaining, this is the best possible grade that can emerge. Grades A and B solutions are rarely entertained because the participants rarely get inside the problem. They only trade demands. An example of a Grade C solution is when negotiators trade off one working condition for another working condition. The company wins one; the union wins the other.

• **Grade D—Solutions Based on Separate Interests in Unrelated Problems.** External constituencies almost never understand Grade D solutions. For example, in one negotiation, the solution consisted of a trade-off between the company and union. It gave the company additional flexibility in a working condition in exchange for additional days off for the unionized employees. The external constituencies did not understand the trade-off. Instead, they analyzed the agreement as a victory for the company on flexibility and a victory for the union on days off. Each negotiator won one case and lost the other. The connection between the separate interests in a Grade D solution is too tenuous for external constituencies to see any relationship between them.

What Happens if Even a Grade "D" Solution Cannot Be Agreed Upon?

If negotiators cannot resolve a problem within these four grades of problem resolution, then they have failed the interest approach course. The negotiations will regress to a rights or power approach.

As a last chance to "pass the course" before resorting to the rights approach, the negotiators can ask themselves a series of questions together or separately. These are:

- Is this a zero-sum negotiation? Is there any way to increase the available resources—that is, expand the pie? (Traditional negotiators shrink the pie, while mutual gains negotiators know how to expand the pie.)

- Are there any areas of the problem in which you have reached agreement? Identify those areas of agreement and specify the unresolved parts of the problem.

- What solution would an unbiased mediator suggest for the part of the problem that is unresolved?

- What would the more favorable solution be from a mediator who was biased for one side or the other?

Perhaps by answering these questions the parties may generate solutions together without having to resort to the legal process or use a third party to adjudicate. If this fails, then the rights approach commences. If the rights intervention also fails, then each party will have to decide what it will do unilaterally with this problem. Is it worth fighting over, or do you let this problem go unresolved?

Generally, negotiators should not be too stubborn over an article in an agreement if it will block concluding the collective agreement. The only time to take a stand is when the battle is over a principle.

For example, in one negotiation the union wanted to index pensions. The company was prepared to take a strike because the union was introducing a new concept—a new principle that they would have to endure permanently. The union chief spokesperson realized the resistance was due to the introduction of the new principle, not the additional money. In the end they were able to settle for a few pennies more, and the principle was not included in the collective agreement. The union leadership concluded that in the tough economic times of that year, it was more important to keep the workers employed than to strike based upon an indexing pension principle.

THIS IS NOT MERLIN . . . NO ONE IS SELLING MAGIC WANDS

The negotiating parties need to recognize that although mutual gains negotiating works very well and can contribute to union-management peace, it may not resolve all problems. It is a probability exercise. The chance of a mutual gains agreement is much higher than with adversarial bargaining, but it also may not work. In mutual gains negotiations, taking a position is sometimes part of the process.

Three situations in which taking a position and/or saying "no" might occur are:

• **The problems that are presented are radical ideas that can never be considered by one side or the other.** Even in mutual gains negotiations, parties are sometimes unwilling to consider a radical problem. In those cases, one party said "no." Sometimes "no" is said in more humorous ways. As when the company proposed the introduction of pay for performance and the union representative retorted: "I object. I cannot afford to live on that." If the trust is higher, then at least that party should allow counterparts to explain why there is a need to explore the idea. At the outset, however, one party can say no where appropriate and it should not terminate the mutual gains negotiations process for other issues.

• **The two parties still may not agree after negotiating a problem.** Invariably, if they went through the entire process, their differences are narrowed; however, they still may not have achieved an agreed-upon solution. At that point, it is appropriate for each side to state its position on the issue. The parties may engage in traditional negotiations to reach compromise between the two positions, which will probably require mutual concessions.

• **Many negotiators have found that it is more difficult to apply the mutual gains process to the monetary packages of a collective agreement.** Typically, this is true if there are fewer variables to put into the overall monetary package equation. For example, if all that can be negotiated is the salary per hour, then it will be a "push and pull" situation in which one will want more and the other will want to give less. On the other hand, if the variables include salary, benefits, pension, vacation, sick leave, and so on, then the total dollar value per hour worked can be assessed. In addition, each individual line may be adjusted to potentially produce an equation that meets the needs of both the employer and the union.

However, if the monetary negotiations proceed in a demand/counterdemand manner, it is not a failure of the mutual gains negotiations process. It simply reflects that the process was beneficial to many issues but did not contribute added value to one part of the overall negotiations. After contract negotiations, the ongoing dialogue usually focuses on working conditions issues. Even if the negotiators apply mutual gains negotiating only to the working conditions issues in contract negotiations, they probably will be able to use it in administering the contract after it is ratified.

PUTTING THE COLLECTIVE AGREEMENT INTO ACTION

After signing the collective agreement, phase 5, the most difficult phase, begins. The agreement is not the end of the union-management peace process; it is the beginning. The parties need to find mechanisms to ensure that management and unionized employees will operate in accordance with the intent and specifics of their agreement. Also, they need to identify a method of continuous dialogue to review decisions that both parties believe are not working well.

During the term of an agreement, many opportunities occur for parties to fall out of trust. When this happens, the parties should consider other alternative dispute resolution processes. For example, one company and union agreed to internal arbitration to resolve disputes before going through formal arbitration.

If the parties include a values and principles section in the agreement, they should strongly emphasize this section. Mechanisms that ensure that employees live by those values and principles on a day-to-day basis should be supported in all learning experiences within the company and the union.

Parties should anticipate that there will be mistakes. The willingness to forgive and foster recovery is important to ensure a new lifestyle for the company and its union. Past problems may have occurred, but for parties to keep moving from where they are to where they need to be, a new order needs to emerge. Mutual gains negotiations is one of the major characteristics of that new way of working together to achieve union-management peace.

Companies and unions have used many other effective strategies. Some of these include:

- Engage in a joint communication process after the completion of negotiations to educate everyone about the new agreement.

- Conduct a joint union-management debriefing meeting to review the strengths and weaknesses of this round of negotiations and to consider strategies to make the implementation of the new contract as successful as possible. The parties can determine an overall "grade" for the negotiations.

- Develop joint union-management councils that will engage in ongoing dialogue and problem resolution about issues related to union-management relations.

- Provide joint training for union leadership and management on mutual gains problem solving so that the approach used in contract negotiations will become the ongoing style of communication between union leadership and management. In addition, encourage management to use the mutual gains negotiating style as the new management style within the company.

- Put the agreement and its intent into operation in everything that is done. Each grievance is another opportunity to apply mutual gains problem solving before it escalates to arbitration.

Any idea that supports the operation of union-management peace needs to be explored. As parties work together and build trust in each other, the benefits will be exponential for them, as is described in Chapter 10. In many respects, unions and companies are entering into uncharted territory. The opportunities are vast if they are willing to take advantage of them.

SUMMARY

- Some useful guidelines that help negotiators reach mutual gains agreements include the following:
  - Do not let desperation be your inspiration.
  - An agreement that is good enough today is good enough tomorrow.
  - A good deal sells itself.
  - Nothing is binding until agreement.
- Traditionally, parties write the language after they sign a memorandum and reach an agreement. Typically, management writes the language, often under great time pressure. It is not surprising that occasionally the language does not accurately reflect what was really negotiated.
- When a company writes the contract after the negotiations, we recommend that at least one union negotiator attend the writing sessions so that the company will reflect the intent of the agreement in the contract.
- There are some crucial steps to consider before signing a collective labor agreement:
  - Do a complete costing of the collective agreement.

- Develop a list of "killer questions" from the perspective of the key stakeholders who will review the agreement.

- Make a decision that the mutual gains agreement is equal to or better than what parties would have negotiated through the rights or power approaches.

- Presell the agreement to some of the key influencers to increase the likelihood that key constituencies understand and accept it.

• In almost every case, the parties need to consult the key stakeholders before they reach an agreement. In the union, the national representatives are often the stakeholders who need input, while within the company, the senior executive often becomes involved.

• Mutual gains solutions are commonly far more creative than the kinds of solutions you see traditionally. This may surprise some key stakeholders.

• Keeping stakeholders apprised of developments may be useful so that they are able to work with the negotiators at the final stages of negotiations.

• In mutual gains negotiating, when the parties are at the point of reaching agreement, they discuss the mechanisms that will support the new contract.

• Some strategies companies and unions have used successfully to ensure that their people incorporate the values and principles adhered to in the negotiations are:

- Ensure that the principles and values demonstrated in the negotiations process become part of the collective labor agreement.

- Develop joint union-management teams within the company that will deal with ongoing union-management problem solving.

- Engage in joint union-management training in the area of joint problem solving.

- Companies and unions have used the new contract, which includes values and intent as well as principles, to introduce a new way of working within the company.
- All negotiators sign the agreement, demonstrating their 100 percent commitment to what they negotiated. Once they sign it, they own the entire agreement even if they have difficulty with parts it.
- After the union signs the agreement, they bring it to the membership for a vote. On the company side, the senior executive waits for the union to approve the agreement.
- With the approvals in place, the parties can ratify the agreement and then celebrate.
- With the celebration complete, the agreement should be published quickly.
- At the conclusion of negotiations, all negotiators should be present to do a process review.
- The next step is to communicate and educate all employees about the new agreement.
- Evaluation is an essential component of any negotiation.
- Some of the self-evaluation methods used include:
  - Identifying whether the solutions are wise, simple, and enhance the relationship.
  - Determining which of the stakeholders will be the winners, losers, and accidental losers.
  - Using a grading system.
- There are four grade levels in mutual gains negotiations:
  - Grade A—Solutions based on common interests within the problem.
  - Grade B—Solutions based on common interests and separate interests within the problem.

- – Grade C—Solutions based on separate interests in related problems.
- – Grade D—Solutions based on separate interests in unrelated problems.
- If negotiators cannot resolve a problem within these four grades of problem resolution, then they failed the interest approach course. The negotiations will regress to a rights or power approach.
- After signing the collective agreement, the most difficult part actually begins. The parties need to find mechanisms to ensure that management and unionized employees will operate in accordance with the intent and specifics of their agreement. Also, they need to identify a method of continuous dialogue to review decisions that both parties believe are not working well.

CHAPTER 9

Negotiation Traps

An autocratic boss took his best employee on a fishing trip to try to repair their relationship. They were fishing not far from shore when the boss said, "I want to go back and get a beer." The employee immediately started the motor, but the boss said, "Don't bother. I'll just walk to the shore." The employee was stunned as the boss climbed out of the boat and started walking on the water—and then sank to the bottom of the river. Without hesitation, the employee dove into the water, brought the boss to shore and saved him by administering artificial respiration. As the boss came to, he said, "Thank you for saving my life, but please do me a favor—don't tell anyone I couldn't walk on water." To which the employee immediately replied, "On one condition. I won't tell anyone that you couldn't walk on water, if you won't tell anyone I saved you!"

Mutual gains solutions can be found even in the most unusual circumstances, yet there are numerous ways that something good can be sabotaged. In negotiations, hidden traps must be tracked and avoided. There are at least seven "negotiation" traps that prevent and sabotage union-management peace. If negotiators fall into one or more of these traps, the opportunity to achieve peace and agreement may be lost or derailed.

To do something right, it is helpful to study what can go wrong. The field of medicine began making quantum leaps when doctors started doing autopsies. They could discover their mistakes and, in their case, literally bury them. Those who do not learn from their mistakes are doomed to repeat them. Hopefully, this chapter will help the reader sidestep some of the major barriers and traps to mutual gains success.

One important strategy that is not a trap is to experiment with mutual gains negotiations. By trying this process, the negotiating parties lose nothing except time. They also realize that they can always revert to the old methods and exercise their rights and power. The benefit is that participants will be able to say with integrity that they tried. In most cases, the willingness to give peace an honest opportunity for success is the first step toward the beginning of a new union-management relationship.

The following are the seven negotiation traps and strategies for recognizing and responding to them:

NEGOTIATION TRAP 1—ONE OF THE PARTIES RESISTS MUTUAL GAINS NEGOTIATIONS

This trap is perhaps the most common problem in mutual gains negotiations. Perhaps it is as one labor lawyer said: "Industrial relations are like sexual relations, better between consenting adults."

To avoid this trap, you must discover why parties resist using mutual gains negotiations. There are many reasons, including the following:

- **Parties think mutual gains negotiating is a trick.** If parties have experienced negotiations in the past that were filled with tricks, these experiences may influence their beliefs about mutual gains negotiations. They could appropriately assume that the other party's interest in mutual gains negotiations is a trick to make them believe the approach will be mutually beneficial.

- **When stakes are very high (i.e. during contract negotiations), parties do not understand why it is necessary to use an entirely different approach.** If the mutual gains approach was not used when the previous contract was negotiated, parties have a valid point in asking why they should use this approach for a current contract.

- **If a party's day-to-day interactions are inconsistent with the mutual gains approach, it will be difficult for that party to convince counterparts that they want to participate in mutual gains negotiating.** The discontinuity between the negotiating method and the party's normal actions is jarring. Therefore, it is difficult to believe that the party actually desires to engage in mutual gains negotiations.

- **Parties are satisfied with the results of the old way of negotiating.** They question why they should try a new way when the old way has worked so well for them.

- **Parties are unable to forgive their counterparts for past injustices.** They negotiate through the "rearview mirror." This means they negotiate the next contract by looking at the injustices of the past. They use this negotiation to "make whole" or repay the outstanding debt they believe is owed to them.

These challenges are very strong and, in some cases, cannot be overcome. The desire for union-management peace may take longer than anticipated. The mutual gains approach may have to be rolled out slowly, perhaps after the current round of negotiations when the stakes are lower and possibly over two contract periods.

Strategies to Respond to Negotiation Trap 1

The following are some of the strategies that have convinced a resistant party to try mutual gains negotiations:

1. **Find "soft" opportunities to educate the party.** Attend union-management conferences on the topic of mutual gains negotiations. Invite the party to visit other companies and/or unions with you or by themselves to ask questions about the mutual gains working environment.

2. **Engage in joint mutual gains negotiations training that is nonbinding.** Resistant parties may be willing to engage in joint mutual gains negotiation training if it is nonbinding. By participating in training, they gain an in-depth look at the new approach. It is also an opportunity to build and perhaps repair relationships that need mending. All the principal negotiators should be present, even the ones who are often resistant.

3. **Agree on external facilitation the first time with this new process.** Suggest that the resistant party identify three candidates who have functioned as neutral external facilitators. Explain that you will choose one from their list. People do not argue with their own data. If they propose the facilitator, they will be more likely to accept that person as the orchestrator of the process.

4. **Avoid labeling the negotiation method with a fancy name like mutual gains negotiations.** In some cases a name of a process generates resistance, as described in Chapter 5. Identify the process as joint problem-solving or simply effective negotiations, or give it no name at all.

5. **Just do it.** In one contentious situation during a training session, two hard-nosed company negotiators had to attend a pregrievance meeting with union representatives who were not participating in the training. The meeting was held during the evening of one of the days of joint training. The company representatives intended to go to the meeting and use a power approach to get what they wanted. Instead, they decided to try the new approach they were learning in training. Without any introduction or explanation, they asked their counterparts why the company suggestion was so problematic for them. The two parties then identified their common interests and began non-binding brainstorming. To everyone's surprise, they discovered a mutual gains solution.

The next day the two company negotiators returned to the joint training room beaming. They told the story of their success, which was based upon an agreement not to apply seniority to a specific case and to document it as nonprecedent-setting. The union had been concerned about precedent setting; management wanted the case resolved. By "just doing it," they resolved the case to everyone's satisfaction.

6. **Negotiate the ground rules (principles) and sign a negotiations contract that will apply throughout the mutual gains negotiations.** The agreement can include the method by which negotiations will proceed as well as the logistics for negotiations, such as who pays what, the duration of negotiations, and how to opt out of the process. Clear escape clauses provide the necessary comfort for parties to enter into negotiations without fear that they can never get out. (A more elaborate discussion of negotiating principles appears in Chapter 5.)

7. **Use every opportunity to demonstrate that you are serious about a new kind of relationship with your counterpart.** Be honest and keep channels of communication open. Notice any signal that the other party's resistance to mutual gains negotiations is softening and capitalize on the moment. Your counterpart may engage in mutual gains discussion unintentionally. A positive experience from this discussion may result in the party exploring the mutual gains approach the next time a dispute needs resolution.

8. **As a last resort, you may have to let the negotiations reach the boiling point before your counterpart will consider mutual gains negotiations.** Techniques that can be used under these conditions are:

- Establish at the beginning that you will not consider any demand unless the other party is willing to tell you why it is important.

- Do not give in to threats; deal with the threatening act, not the content of the threat. If you do give in to a threat, get ready for "BOHICA," or "Bend over; here it comes again."

- If your counterpart gives a long list of demands, you can respond with utopian demands of your own to counteract the positional bargaining. The rule of thumb is "tit for tat."[18] Do not exceed your counterpart's aggressiveness but be able to counteract it or match it.

- Continue to look for opportunities to use a mutual gains approach after the boiling point is reached.

NEGOTIATION TRAP 2—USING MUTUAL GAINS NEGOTIATIONS AS A SOURCE OF POWER

There are two kinds of power attacks. One is an attack by an obvious aggressor. You see the imminent danger and attempt to defend yourself. The second is more subtle. Your counterpart attacks you without your realizing you are being attacked. You are defenseless to the alternative source of power.

As with any good thing, mutual gains negotiating can be misused. For example, one union agreed to participate in mutual gains negotiations as an alternate method of delaying government involvement in the negotiations. They used a filibuster technique to ensure that no substantial problems were ever completely addressed. In another case, a company introduced mutual gains only to resort to ultimatums when it became clear that the monetary package exceeded its mandate. The change in approach disabled the union and they responded slowly. Typically, in adversarial bargaining, the union mobilization of membership would be taking place over the course of negotiations. In this example, the union found it hard to mobilize the membership quickly to take on a traditional fight after doing mutual gains negotiating.

Strategies to Respond to Negotiation Trap 2

Some of the approaches for disarming Negotiation Trap 1 apply to this trap as well. The two traps are similar—one party wants to use mutual gains negotiations and the other does not. However, in Negotiation Trap 1 the resistant party is obvious about not wanting to participate, and in Negotiation Trap 2 the resistant party uses more subtle methods to demonstrate resistance.

1. Useful strategies for avoiding Negotiation Trap 2 are to train parties jointly, use an external facilitator, develop documented negotiating principles, do not label the process, and "just do it."

2. Another technique that may be useful is a structured process of **"gate reviews."** The technology of gate reviews is taken from effective project management. The parties build periodic reviews into the negotiations process, during which they modify how they are operating and agree to continue negotiating using mutual gains negotiations. In the review process, the parties have to make a series of decisions (pass through a series of gates) as represented in Figure 9–1.

F I G U R E   9 – 1

Gate Review Process

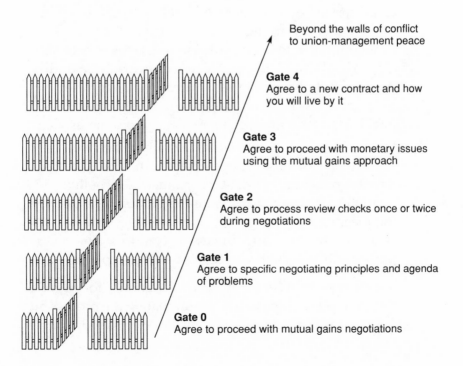

Beyond the walls of conflict
to union-management peace

Gate 4
Agree to a new contract and how
you will live by it

Gate 3
Agree to proceed with monetary issues
using the mutual gains approach

Gate 2
Agree to process review checks once or twice
during negotiations

Gate 1
Agree to specific negotiating principles and agenda
of problems

Gate 0
Agree to proceed with mutual gains negotiations

These gates provide a structured method for reducing manipulation of the process and for guiding the negotiating parties *beyond the walls of conflict.*

- *Gate 0—Agree to proceed with mutual gains negotiations.* Parties usually agree upon Gate 0 after the joint training.

- *Gate 1—Agree to specific negotiating principles to which the parties will conform and an agenda of problems that will be the content of the contract negotiations.* This is usually agreed upon during the first few weeks of face-to-face negotiations.

- *Gate 2—Agree to a process review, perhaps once or twice during the negotiations.* Passing through Gate 2 means the parties are willing to continue with the mutual gains approach for the next stage of negotiations.

- *Gate 3—Agree to proceed with the monetary issues using the mutual gains approach.* Monetary concerns are often characterized by management wanting to give very little and the union wanting to get as much as they can. In some mutual gains negotiations, the parties decide to skip Gate 3 and negotiate the monetary package traditionally. If they agree to use mutual gains for this segment of the negotiations, they will enhance the likelihood of a mutual gains monetary solution as well.

- *Gate 4—Agree on a new contract.* In most collective bargaining sessions, the agreement is the only gate the parties go through. It can be expanded with both a debriefing meeting and a planning process. The debriefing meeting is to review and evaluate the entire negotiations, and the planning process is to address how the parties will live by the agreement after it is put in place.

The gate review process can be used not only for negotiations in which one side seems to be manipulating the process but for all negotiations. It is particularly useful for Negotiation Trap 2.

This is because gate reviews break the larger negotiation into a series of smaller, discreet negotiations that reduce the parties' resistance and/or ability to manipulate the entire process.

NEGOTIATION TRAP 3—NEGOTIATING WITH AMATEURS

In any negotiation situation, the most difficult people to negotiate with are amateurs. Amateurs think they know it all. You do not know what they will do next because they do not know either. In a recent negotiation, an external mediator was dealing with a major negotiation between a company and a large trade union. The union negotiators were rookies—amateurs in negotiations. At the beginning of the negotiations, one of the union negotiators stood on a chair and sang the Engelbert Humperdink song, "Please Release Me Let Me Go." After he finished, the mediator said: "Let me tell you three things: number one, you cannot sing; number two, you do not understand the process; and number three, I can embarrass you at any time."

The mediator gave the amateur a quick education. Although it was an unorthodox technique, it worked. After that incident, the trade unionist would do anything to please the mediator—even shine his shoes if he asked for it.

Amateurs show a wide range of behaviors. Some may be hostile and mistrustful. They may believe they will be hurt through negotiations and then they will be blamed. They may demonstrate false bravado by inappropriate yelling and swearing. Other amateurs paint themselves into a corner and do not know how to get out. It is very tempting for the experienced negotiator to take advantage of this weakness and to structure agreements that the amateur negotiator's constituencies will see as a sellout. That kind of aggressiveness, although tempting, may come back to haunt negotiators. If a party beats its opposition too badly, there will undoubtedly be a new negotiator the next time with the mandate to strike revenge. Negotiators should consider alternative strategies.

Strategies to Respond to Negotiation Trap 3

Many strategies have worked successfully. These include the following:

1. **Educate them—get them into joint training.** If they are unwilling to participate in joint training, ask them to join you at a union-management conference that has educational components. Give them a chance to speak with colleagues at the conference who may know more then they do.

2. **Establish credibility with your counterpart.** Work on building the relationship. Always be available to talk to anyone, anytime, and at any place. Find opportunities to consider the counterpart's perspective rather than just your own when dealing with problems.

3. **Break down negotiations into small committees.** Use a joint committee approach to explore different problems. Using small teams will help build relationships and reduce the theatrics amateurs often display.

4. **Find confidence builders.** Look for opportunities to build the confidence of the amateurs with early joint successes. Work on the general issues first or the ones in which many common interests are likely. Through early positive experiences, the amateur will learn how to negotiate, and the relationship will begin to be built to sustain you through more complex problems.

5. **Perhaps wait until the negotiations reach a boiling point and then amateurs may be willing to work with you to resolve the pressure.** They may even be willing to tell you what they are doing—if they know.

NEGOTIATION TRAP 4—THE TWO NEGOTIATING PARTIES WANT TO BE ONE TEAM

In this situation, the parties' wishes are very different from those in previous negotiation traps. Instead of personal interests governing the way they negotiate, their desire is to be one team. In some cases that kind of unity can be advantageous; however, the parties always need to be aware of their differences as well as their similarities as they negotiate.

Negotiators who place the team above all else on a regular basis can be vulnerable to the "crisis of agreement." In his book on ethical management, *The Abilene Paradox,* Jerry Harvey points out that sometimes organizations suffer from the crisis of agreement more than from the crisis of conflict.[19] Negotiating parties who want to be one team can be vulnerable to the crisis of agreement. The example of the shortened work week solution (p. 176) in which the parties forgot the customer's needs illustrates the crisis of agreement phenomenon.

The term "team" should be understood by negotiating parties. "Team" is a word that is overused to the point of meaninglessness. Essentially, a team is erroneously considered to be any group consisting of more than one person. A more accurate definition is "a group that has mutual accountabilities." To be worthy of being called a team, all the team members should be measured by the same results.

Strategies to Respond to Negotiation Trap 4

The negotiators can agree to several mutual accountabilities. These include achieving a grade "A" or grade "B" in their negotiations, which means that they build their agreement around the common and separate interests in the problems. Other negotiators identify the mutual accountability of achieving a mutual gains agreement without a work stoppage. However, there will always be differences between the parties because of the constituencies the parties represent and because of their separate interests.

The two negotiating parties often face different realities of the business from the perspectives of the constituencies they represent. Situations that are outside the mandate of one of the negotiators can damage the credibility of the mutual gains process. These are circumstances such as hostile takeovers of the union or the company, loss of market share, change in leadership, and external pressures to reach agreements. An excellent team of negotiators may be able to withstand those pressures; however, all parties must realize that these pressures can pull them apart and dissolve the unity of the team.

Mature negotiators may be able to respect their differences and at the same time introduce some strategies to solidify their gains with each other. Some techniques include:

1. **Write the intent of their contract into the collective agreement so that the next generation of negotiators will be able to follow the pattern set by these negotiators.** This strategy is one of the key success factors of mutual gains negotiations.

2. **Consider moving negotiations from an event that occurs every two to three years to continuous dialogue with a moratorium on the monetary package.**

3. **Ensure that the management style emulates the negotiating style used in collective bargaining and continuous dialogue.** If the corporate culture changes to be consistent with the mutual gains negotiating style, then the ability to persevere during difficult times will be improved.

NEGOTIATION TRAP 5—THE NEGOTIATING PARTY IS TOO QUICK TO RESORT TO OLD HABITS

One negotiator referred to the mutual gains negotiations process as "two steps forward and one step back." There are many bumps in the road to mutual gains solutions. Some negotiators regress by resorting to power too quickly instead of as a last resort. Others regress in more subtle ways. Some may manipulate inadvertently. Others may start taking the negotiations very personally or play people off each other rather than dealing with the issues, while still others may focus only on demands and not explore interests.

Strategies to Respond to Negotiation Trap 5

Strategies that may be helpful to reduce the impact of the regression to old habits include:

1. **Normalize the regression to old habits as natural.** People do not change old habits overnight. It is understandable to fall back into traditional ways of doing things, even without knowing it. Label it as normal, identify it when it occurs, and gain commitment to continue to try to use the negotiating principles to regress less frequently.

In one negotiation, the union and the company found it was difficult not to swear during negotiations even though they had established no swearing as a negotiation principle. The astute facilitator realized the dilemma. Rather than insist that the parties fight the desire to be nasty from time to time, he built it into the negotiations process. He set his watch on a 58-minute countdown feature, and after 58 minutes his watch beeper went off. For a period of two minutes, the negotiating parties were allowed to scream at each other, swear, say anything they liked. The noise and laughter as they did this was terrific relationship building. After the two minutes, the groups returned to another period of mutual gains discussions.

2. **Use the joint training to teach the parties how to do gate reviews, and then use that capability during negotiations.** (Gate reviews are described in Negotiation Trap 2.)

3. **If a negative pattern is emerging that is not covered by the original negotiation principles, review the principles during negotiations.** Gain agreement from the group to expand the negotiation principles to include ending the destructive negotiating behavior.

4. **If two people have a personality conflict, they should settle their personal differences off-line, that is, not with the entire group present.** If the parties are using an external facilitator, that person can facilitate the discussion. Informal ground rules can be developed between the two disputants to ensure they can continue to negotiate with each other in a civil manner.

NEGOTIATION TRAP 6—LACK OF SENIOR LEADERSHIP BUY-IN

Senior leadership may not support the mutual gains process for many reasons. The negotiations may be a high risk for them, and people are often very wary of risking the entire enterprise on a new process. The approach of having only people of low authority as negotiators will produce benefits with little impact. Getting senior leadership buy-in is worth the effort.

The characteristics of senior leaders may be useful to consider as you solicit their support. These are some examples of problematic leadership styles from a humorous perspective:

- **The "Ostrich."** Ostriches keep their heads in the sand and do not see danger approaching. They know nothing about the potential of mutual gains negotiations and will do little to find out about it. It is said about them that "you should never attribute to conspiracy that which can be equally attributed to incompetence."

- **The "Mushroom."** Mushrooms are kept in the dark and fed fertilizer to make them grow. Leaders who treat people as mushrooms will resist sharing facts they see as their power base. They need tangible results before they are willing to consider this approach.

- **The "Owl" (taken from the "Owl and the Centipede" story in Chapter 8).** Owls assume they have all the wisdom and that the negotiators should do what they say and nothing else. It is said that "their little decisions made at 70,000 feet will make a hell of a lot of noise when they hit the ground." These leaders set specific targets and expectations for negotiations and demand that the negotiators deliver what they want.

- **The "Crab."** Crabs like to create an environment in which everyone is trying to climb up and out of the pail, only to have another crab pull them back just as they are about to get out. The internal competition in the organization is fierce and exists by design as a warped perspective on how to motivate people. Crabs welcome adversarial union management negotiations as another expression of the way they like to lead.

- **The "Frog."** Frogs will sit in cold water, and as it starts to boil will remain in the water until they die. They are aware of what is going on around them, but they never gain sufficient perspective to recognize the need to change their direction.

Each of these styles is problematic. Without support from senior leadership, very few decisions can be made at the negotiating table, and extensive delays will occur as senior leaders mull over decisions. Major problems will also occur when the negotiators try to sell the mutual gains agreement to them.

In one negotiation, senior leadership indifference to the negotiations process was reflected in an 80 percent turnover of the company negotiating team. The senior leadership repeatedly removed the negotiators from the negotiations to work on other projects they felt were of greater importance. The lack of continuity in negotiators sabotaged a valiant attempt to create a new union-management relationship.

Strategies to Respond to Negotiation Trap 6

Some strategies that have been effective in creating senior leadership buy-in include the following:

1. **Find a way to involve leadership in some mutual gains negotiations training.** Usually, leaders are willing to participate

in a briefing session to inform them about the style of the upcoming negotiations.

2. **Have leadership invest money in the negotiations training and the negotiations process itself.** The investment of money usually gets their attention.

3. **Maximize access routes to the senior leadership.** In the creativity section (Chapter 7) of this book, finding new access routes is described as a creative technique. It works with resistant senior leadership as well. Usually, you will need as many as four access routes to have them reduce their resistance. Some access routes include:

- Talk to senior leadership directly.
- Ask an external authority figure in negotiations to present to them.
- Have another senior leader they respect influence them.
- Ask other organizations that use mutual gains to engage in dialogue with them.
- Expose them to resources for their review such as external experts, professional journals, and periodicals on mutual gains negotiating.

4. **Communicate in their language.** This means that if they think in political, financial, or personal gains terms, structure your influence strategies in their language to meet their interests. Talk in terms of financial benefits to the senior leader who is only concerned about the bottom line; talk in terms of political success to the leader who is only concerned about reelection or promotion.

5. **Communicate during leadership's low-stress times.** Find out when they are more willing to listen to people. Sometimes it is over breakfast; sometimes it is later in the day; but communicate when they are most receptive.

6. **See yourself as a colleague and not as a subordinate.** Many people are nervous around senior leadership and show it in the way they approach them and speak to them. Visualize

yourself as the senior leaders' equal. How would you talk with them as an equal? How would you talk to them if you were their senior leader? Would you change your tone, provide more of your insights about what to do, be more direct? All these may work in the process of influencing senior leadership.

7. **Use the gate review process to manage the negotiations.** The gate review meeting (described in Negotiation Trap 2) can be an opportunity to meet with the senior leadership to discuss progress in negotiations. The periodic gate review meetings will also justify not talking to the senior leadership between the gate reviews.

8. **As a last resort, try strategic avoidance.** Although this is not the preferred strategy, it may be better at times to keep senior leadership uninformed, especially if they are the "ostrich," "mushroom," or "crab" leaders. You may be better off apologizing for not informing them rather than asking for their permission. When you do approach them, bring some tangible evidence that the approach yields benefits.

NEGOTIATION TRAP 7—DISCONTINUITY WITH DAY-TO-DAY UNION-MANAGEMENT RELATIONSHIPS

The mutual gains approach is more than a technique or a useful tool; it is a change in the mind-set, a change in the culture of the enterprise. If it remains on the level of a technique, the full value of this approach will not be realized and union-management peace will be elusive.

In one situation management participated in joint training with the union. The union saw the mutual gains approach as a new lifestyle to be used in every encounter and relationship. The company saw it as a new technique, an alternate style of negotiating.

The union struggled with the lack of investment by the company in changing the style of management to the mutual gains problem-solving approach. They believed that this style of negotiation would be effective as an ongoing management style. The company saw this approach as isolated to the negotiations of the collective labor agreement and not applicable to general management.

The company began suffering from a credibility gap. Why was this approach good enough for contract negotiations and not good enough as a management style? The discontinuity between what the employees experienced on a day-to-day basis and what management was trying to do in negotiations was too great. Management's desire to participate in mutual gains negotiations was not taken seriously.

Strategies to Respond to Negotiation Trap 7

Every relationship in the organization needs a total commitment to mutual gains negotiations and problem solving. In some organizations mutual gains negotiating is an alternate access route to total quality, with full collaboration with the union.

If the company or the union does not support wise solutions that are simple and that enhance the relationships in all problem-solving situations, their intentions will be questioned. If the company or union does not consistently apply mutual gains negotiations and reverts regularly to adversarial approaches, their credibility as mutual gains negotiators will be in doubt.

Some essential strategies to incorporating mutual gains negotiations into the daily work life in an organization are described below:

1. **The company and the union leadership must make mutual gains negotiations and problem solving a new way of life.** The senior leadership should serve as models in this culture-changing process.

2. **The new leadership role is as a facilitator of mutual gains problem solving.** Leadership should apply this approach regularly to every encounter with employees, managers, and the union.

3. **Managers' ability to function as mutual gains problem solvers should be assessed by peers, employees, and supervisors.** This capability should be measured and rewarded so that it will be taken seriously.

4. **Consider changing the culture in the organization to a mutual gains culture at the same time (or even before) you change the nature of collective bargaining.** If collective negotiation leads the way in the mutual gains experiment, be sure to quickly follow up by implementing mutual gains training for managers and unionized employees so that it becomes part of the daily fabric of the organization.

5. **Design management-union teams that will use mutual gains problem solving and will work together in continuous dialogue on issues of interest to all parties throughout the collective agreement.** Give these groups the mandate to make decisions and operate autonomously to benefit employees and the work unit.

6. **Publicize success stories to create continuous learning from other experiences and to constantly reinforce the commitment to a mutual gains culture.**

SUMMARY

- This chapter identifies seven traps that prevent union-management peace and strategies for avoiding these traps:
  - Negotiation Trap 1—One of the Parties Resists Mutual Gains Negotiations.
  - Negotiation Trap 2—Using Mutual Gains Negotiations as a Source of Power.
  - Negotiation Trap 3—Negotiating with Amateurs.
  - Negotiation Trap 4—The Two Negotiating Parties Want to Be One Team.
  - Negotiation Trap 5—The Negotiating Party Is Too Quick to Resort to Old Habits.

- Negotiation Trap 6—Lack of Senior Leadership Buy-In.
- Negotiation Trap 7—Discontinuity with Day-to-Day Union-Management Relationships.

CHAPTER 10

Beyond the Walls
of Conflict

The biggest challenge to union-management peace is to move *beyond the walls of conflict* after contract negotiations. The approaches, techniques, and solutions described in this book are very useful during mutual gains negotiations. However, for stakeholders to realize the longer-term benefits of the process they need to experiment with a new kind of relationship of union-management peace as a way of life.

For it to fulfill its potential, union-management peace cannot be something that occurs and then passes. It must be a state of being, a mind-set. It must be evident in the work setting and expand into one's personal life.

For example, one union negotiator returned to a union-management meeting elated about a success he had had at home the evening before. He had decided to try creating peace in his home through mutual gains negotiating. He and his son had been in serious conflict for a few years, and the father was about to throw his son out of the house. That evening he decided to explore his son's interests and express his own interests. They found that they had more in common than they thought. One common interest was that they both wanted to figure out a way for the son not to have to leave home.

After some brainstorming, they had finally agreed to specific ground rules. While the rules did not include everything that each wanted, they met their common interests. Most importantly, father and son had found some peace, which had eluded them for a long time. The union negotiator was shocked at how easy it was to apply what he had learned in collective bargaining to his home environment.

I had a somewhat similar experience. I was sitting in a restaurant in New Jersey with my three-and-a-half-year-old son on our first vacation together. We had been driving for two hours. We sat down to eat and I was encouraging my son to eat his food and finish his plate. He looked at me and said, "Daddy, 'no' is 'no.' " Quite surprised, I asked him what he meant. He said, in effect, that if we were going to get along on the trip, I must not ask him to eat if he said he did not want to eat.

I tried mutual gains negotiations. I agreed with him on two conditions: (1) that "no" was "no" except in danger and (2) that if he made a deal with me to do something, then he would do it. We got along splendidly throughout the trip repeating numerous times that " 'no' is 'no' except in danger and a deal is a deal."

I saw this as proof that mutual gains negotiating can be used with parent-child relationships until I was asked by my son when he was six years old: "Daddy, what's a 'deal'?" He went on to explain that he never understood why we always talked about dealing a deck of cards! At least he understood that " 'no' is 'no' except in danger."

From marital mediation to political negotiations, the mutual gains process described in this book will have applicability and utility. It reflects a different kind of workplace, a different kind of relationship between diverse people, and, more specifically, a transformation of the union-management relationship.

Union-management peace can create a thriving organization that embraces the diverse cultures within it. All the stakeholders are aligned with each other. All parties participate in an adaptive culture in which all benefit from the trust and integrity of the workplace. The organization has meaning beyond products and services, and its importance for its membership surpasses the annual dues that are collected.

J. B. Priestley, the British playwright, perhaps said it best in his July 21, 1940, wartime broadcast called *Postscripts:* "We must stop thinking in terms of property and power and begin thinking in terms of community and creation." What is needed is the continuous dialogue on common-interest solutions with respect for diverse cultures. Union-management peace has become a common interest for companies, unions, and employees and has the potential to achieve, in Priestley's words, "not the dubious pleasure of power, but the maximum opportunities of creation."

CONTINUOUS DIALOGUE ON COMMON-INTEREST SOLUTIONS WITH RESPECT FOR DIVERSE CULTURES

To establish union-management peace as a way of life, a company and union must support and encourage three key elements:

- Continuous dialogue
- Common-interest solutions
- Diverse cultures

The mutual gains negotiations and problem-solving process is a major vehicle for travel toward union-management peace. Specific strategies to do this are described in the last sections of Chapters 8 and 9. However, continuous dialogue on common-interest solutions in diverse cultures is the higher-level vision that will bring the peace to life.

Continuous Dialogue

Union-management peace requires both continuous dialogue and creativity. The word *continuous* in this context implies an ongoing effort to align all constituencies and to keep everyone informed and involved in the direction of the enterprise. Through continuous involvement and renewal, participants are motivated and inspired to do the right things. They achieve wise and simple solutions that continually build employee relationships and strengthen the business for mutual benefit.

"Dialogue" is a conversation to create possibilities. Within dialogue each party attempts to surface underlying assumptions that may not be evident at first glance. It is an attempt to make what is implicit, explicit. Dialogue is essential for a meaningful conversation about interests and to discover the common interests.

Through continuous dialogue, the parties engage in ongoing discussion. Negotiations are not defined by an event in time every two to three years. Working-conditions problems are negotiated throughout the duration of a contract. A moratorium is declared on the monetary package, but all else is part of the continuous dialogue process.

The new reality that is created is not static. It does not occur in a moment and then fade into an abyss. By continuing nurturing peace, unions and management can ensure that it spreads and deepens.

The energy needed to create the new reality will not happen by itself. It requires intense desire by champions of the process, commitment by senior leadership, and diligence and tenacity on their parts to sustain it against the pressures to revert to more adversarial ways.

At all levels of the company and of the union, the parties need to nurture the potential of union-management peace. When it is no longer fed, it will wither away. The trust of union-management peace is as vulnerable as in any relationship.

Common-Interest Solutions

Labor and management develop common-interest solutions through mutual gains negotiations and problem solving. In an organization that supports union-management peace, employees, union, and management continuously discover common interests and build on them to generate creative solutions.

The common interests reflect the mind-set of the members of the organization and are explicit in the contract. When union-management peace is alive, all parties are aligned in a common direction. The shared common interests guide people to make the right decisions even when they are not formally engaged in mutual gains discussions. Parties know the right thing to do independently, and they can rectify mistakes quickly because they clearly understand the intent and direction of the union-management peace.

Diverse Cultures

A characteristic of respect for diverse cultures is the acceptance and nurturing of the uniqueness of all people within the organization. Rank in the organization is not the important variable, as Peter Block asserts in his book about democracy in the workplace entitled *Stewardship*.[20] Respect and integrity are prime for all. Trust is built regularly and is constantly nurtured. Relationships are created based on common interests. Ultimately, adherence to these principles creates an organization with diverse cultures aligned in a common direction.

An organization that lives union-management peace functions with common interests, appreciation of the diverse aspects of its population, and the ability to dialogue and recreate itself continuously. People are committed and motivated to work in the best interest of the organization.

The organization that respects diverse cultures is built on more than the desire to do work. A feeling that people have a connection and commitment to each other bonds the diverse cultures together. This alignment generates untapped creativity, capitalizes on strengths of individuals and the group, and resists external competitive attacks that would weaken the organization. People are fully informed as equal participants in the organization and are trusted with information.

In many cases union and management operate as one team. However, they have the maturity to recognize when each party needs time alone to think through the implications of a direction for their constituencies. Respect for diversity and allowing people to be with their own culture are necessary.

Union and management do not become one culture. Organizations that attempt to create one culture are not recognizing the multiplicity of cultures that people bring to the workplace. People want their diversity acknowledged, recognized, and validated. They do not want it melted away.

Union and management will always answer to different constituencies and, therefore, will reflect the interests of diverse cultures. A joint union-management due process will still exist that deals with situations that are not aligned with the organization's common interests. Nevertheless, when management and union have continuous dialogue they are able most of the time to operate in alignment with common interests, in a shared collaborative climate, and with appreciation for their distinct cultures.

BENEFITS FOR MAJOR STAKEHOLDERS

Moving *beyond the walls of conflict* results in vast benefits to stakeholders. Consider what the company-union-employee relationship would be like if an enduring union-management peace generated the following:

• Employees view the organization as a company of choice where they work for both personal and professional development. Fear is driven out of the organization, which is one of Edward Deming's 14 principles of quality.

• Unions are partners in the creation of the organization. They represent their constituencies and give them a focused voice for issues of concern and opportunity. They are able to generate agreements that meet the needs of their constituencies and further the cause of employees and the company.

• Leadership takes on a new definition. Leaders have the primary responsibility for continuous dialogue on common-interest solutions with respect for diverse cultures. Their mandate is to discover and build the trust and common interests, appreciate and support the diversity of the organization, and find mutual gains solutions to create, re-create, and grow the organization. The result is a high-performance enterprise aligned in a common direction.

• Customers are continuously delighted with the products and services created by such a highly motivated workforce. Their commitment to the company is reciprocated with service excellence that not only delights customers but also amazes them. Customer loyalty is the norm rather than the exception.

• Companies are able to reap profits from their ability to focus on the external competition rather than focusing on the competition within the enterprise. Senior leadership works with the unions as a partner rather than as an adversary. Senior leadership "walks the talk of quality thought."

• Human resources departments become the leaders in the creation of adaptive cultures that are partners with the unions. The adaptive work organization quickly implements new directions. Lead time to bring new services and products to market is essential to the success of the company. The human resources department is acknowledged as a strategic partner in the continuous change and renewal process for the company, the union, and the employees.

• Industrial relations and union negotiators negotiate on behalf of the company and the union using the mutual gains negotiations approach. Rather than a painful experience, negotiations are seen as an ongoing problem-solving process that is constructive and achieves mutual gains. Negotiations are continuous throughout the duration of the contract with a moratorium on the financial aspects of the contract for a period of time. The contract itself is rewritten and appears in a shorter, more readable form. It is written in a language that any employee can understand and interpret, rather than in legal terminology. The contract includes the common interests to which the union, employees, and management subscribe as well as the intent with which the contract will be interpreted and applied.

• Government supports the new initiatives in union-management peace. Rather than dictate policy, they create policy to enable the parties to negotiate their own agreements. They recognize the need for mutual gains to operate in the interest of the public (what ultimately is good for the public) and not just in the public interest (doing what the public wants even if it is not in the long-term interest of the public).

• Shareholders are ready to invest in the company because of its return on investment and its long-term positive approach to employee and union relations. They stay with the company through both the easy and the difficult times. All employees are shareholders of the company, which contributes to their involvement and commitment to the organization.

EPILOGUE

The French writer and philosopher André Gide said: "All this has been said before, but since nobody listened, I'll say it again." Union-management peace is not an option; it is an imperative. Continuous dialogue on common-interest solutions with respect for diverse cultures can be achieved to the benefit of managers, employees, unions, customers, and shareholders. It generates success beyond what anyone previously imagined.

The imperative comes from the reality and intensity of union-management relations. The union-management relationship is an extremely enduring one and, in most cases, more permanent than many marriages. A marriage has two ways in which it can end. The preferred method is usually divorce (the only other choice is death). Union-management relations almost never have the divorce option. The only way of terminating union-management relations is with death.

The adversarial union-management war is to the death. Union-management peace is a chance for life. The choice is yours . . . choose life!

NOTES

1. Thomas A. Kochan and Paul Osterman, *The Mutual Gains Enterprise* (Boston: Harvard Business School Press, 1994).
2. Saul D. Alinsky, *Reveille for Radicals* (New York: Random House, Vintage Books, 1989).
3. A similar set of criteria are identified by Roger Fisher and William Ury, *Getting to Yes* (New York: Penguin Books, 1975), p. 4.
4. The Honourable Alan B. Gold, "Confessions of a Labour Law Man," Presentation to the Ontario Public School Boards' Association, February 19, 1993.
5. Fisher and Ury, *Getting to Yes.*
6. J. Zelinski, Portrait of Mind Star Toys, Inc. v. Samsung Co. (1992), 9 O. R., (3z) 374, 380 (Gen Div).
7. Yehoshaphat Harkabi, *Israel's Fateful Hour* (New York: Harper & Row, 1988).
8. Saul Alinsky, *Rules for Radicals* (New York: Random House, Vintage Books, 1971).
9. Ibid.
10. George Smith, Presentation at Queens University, Kingston, Ontario, October 1994.
11. This concept was explored by Louis B. Barnes, "Managing the Paradox of Organizational Trust," *Harvard Business Review,* March–April 1981, pp. 107–16.

12. Richard E. Walton and Robert B. McKersie, *A Behavioral Theory of Labor Negotiations* (Ithaca, NY: ILR Press, 1965).

13. Bob Harris, Questionnaire developed for Geller, Shedletsky & Weiss.

14. Stephen R. Covey, *Seven Habits of Highly Effective People* (New York: Simon & Schuster, 1989).

15. The Honourable Alan B. Gold, Presentation to Queen's University, Industrial Relations Centre, May 13, 1994.

16. Collective Agreement between Communications, Energy and Paperworkers Union of Canada and Bell Canada, January 5, 1994.

17. Stanley M. Davis and William H. Davidson, *2020 Vision* (New York: Simon and Schuster, 1991).

18. Robert Axelrod, *The Evolution of Cooperation* (New York: Basic Books, 1984).

19. Jerry Harvey, *The Abilene Paradox* (New York: Free Press, 1988).

20. Peter Block, *Stewardship* (San Francisco: Berrett-Koehler, 1993).

SUGGESTED READINGS

Alinsky, Saul D. *Rules For Radicals.* New York: Vintage Books, 1971.

This book and his earlier work entitled, *Reveille for Radicals* (New York: Random House, Vintage Books, 1989), are the classic books on the war side of union-management war and peace.

Axelrod, Robert. *The Evolution Of Cooperation.* New York: Basic Books, 1984.

This book evolved from a series of journal publications that explored the strategy of "tit for tat" in negotiations. It contributes valuable insight into the negotiation bidding process and how to move the offers to a more cooperative approach.

Bazerman, Max H., and Margaret A. Neale. *Negotiating Rationally.* New York: Maxwell Macmillan International, 1992.

This book is a very useful strategy book for union-management negotiations as well as corporate negotiations of any kind.

Cohen-Rosenthal, Edward, and Cynthia E. Burton. *Mutual Gains.* New York: ILR Press, 1993.

In this second addition, the authors explore the many possible mutual gains solutions that can result from applying a collaborative process to union-management negotiations.

The *Getting . . .* books are written for the general audience of
negotiators. The following are all valuable contributions and
very readable on the topic of interest-based negotiations:

Fisher, Roger, and William Ury. *Getting to Yes.* New York: Penguin
Books, 1975.

This is a best seller on the topic and a significant contribution
and explanation of interest-based negotiations.

Fisher, Roger, and Scott Brown. *Getting Together.* New York:
Penguin Books, 1988.

This book focuses on the relationship side of negotiations.

Ury, William; Jeanne M. Brett; and Stephen Goldberg. *Getting
Disputes Resolved.* San Francisco: Jossey-Bass, 1988.

Ury, William. *Getting Past No.* New York: Bantam Press, 1991.

Kochan, Thomas A., and Paul Osterman. *The Mutual Gains Enterprise.*
Boston: Harvard Business School Press, 1994.

This is an outstanding policy contribution to the field. Its
objectives are very different from those of *Beyond the Walls of
Conflict* but it does function as an excellent companion work.

Lewicki, Roy J.; Joseph A. Litterer; John W. Minton; and David M.
Saunders. *Negotiation.* Burr Ridge, IL: Irwin Professional
Publishing, 1994.

The second edition of this book is extremely useful for instruc-
tors and practitioners to understand the concept of distributive
and integrative bargaining in many application areas.

Walton, Richard E., and Robert B. McKersie. *A Behavioral Theory of
Labor Negotiations.* Ithaca, NY: ILR Press, 1965.

This book is the definitive academic text on the topic of "integrative bargaining," or in modern terms, "interest-based" or
"mutual gains" negotiations.

Walton, Richard E.; Joel E. Cutcher-Gershenfeld; and Robert B.
McKersie. *Strategic Negotiations.* Boston: Harvard Business
School Press, 1994.

This book is an excellent companion to *A Behavioral Theory of
Labor Negotiations,* and provides good examples of how to apply
the theory in cases.

INDEX

Dr. David S. Weiss has been providing consulting services in the field of organizational effectiveness and labor management relations for the past 15 years. He walks the fine line between the different interests of unions and companies. He is proud to be equally accepted by both parties and, because of this unique position, he is an ideal choice to resolve disputes.

David is involved in all aspects of labor-management relations. This includes educating union and company representatives in how to proceed with mutual gains negotiations, assisting companies and unions with the planning phase of the process, facilitating the first few weeks of collective bargaining, assisting with problem resolution as the negotiations proceed, and participating in the culmination of negotiations when the agreement is reached.

In addition, David facilitates joint union-management conferences on competitiveness by bringing global experts to the company and the union so that they can hear the same information from reputable sources. He also designs and delivers joint training programs, whereby union and company representatives are trained in how to deliver mutual gains problem solving seminars for their colleagues after collective agreements are reached, to ensure that all parties can live by the new agreement.

Dr. Weiss is a Partner of the Human Resources and Labor Relations consulting firm of Geller, Shedletsky and Weiss. He received his Doctorate from the University of Toronto, has two Masters degrees from Columbia University, is a Senior Fellow of the Industrial Relations Center of Queen's University, and a Past President of the Industrial Organizational Psychology Section of the Ontario Psychological Association.

He provides consulting services to joint groups of union and management representatives and is contracted separately by unions and management to meet their specific needs. He has an in-depth knowledge and understanding of the company and union interface in times of dramatic change.

David is a sought-after speaker, educator, and facilitator. Due to his expertise in his field, he is quoted in the print media and appears on television for comments. He brings an enthusiastic style of facilitating and presenting that motivates participants to apply what he teaches and to experiment with new ways of doing things.

Thank you for choosing Irwin Professional Publishing for your business information needs. If you are part of a corporation, professional association, or government agency, consider our newest option: Irwin Professional Custom Publishing. This allows you to create customized books, manuals, and other materials from your organization's resources, select chapters of our books, or both.

Irwin Professional Publishing books are also excellent resources for training/ educational programs, premiums, and incentives. For information on volume discounts or Custom Publishing, call 1-800-634-3966.

Other books of interest to you from Irwin Professional Publishing . . .

UNIONS, MANAGEMENT AND QUALITY

Opportunities for Innovation and Excellence

Edward Cohen-Rosenthal

Co-published with the Association for Quality and Participation

The first book to address how unions and management can work together to improve a company's quality efforts and maximize performance. Presents examples from leading organizations in manufacturing, service, and public sectors, such as General Motors, the United Autoworkers, and many others.
0-7863-0157-0   275 pages

MINING GROUP GOLD

How to Cash In on the Collaborative Brain Power of a Group

Revised Edition

Thomas A. Kayser

Excellent counsel for anyone interested in changing a corporate culture. Gives five steps for planning and conducting a successful group session; offers suggestions for dealing with feelings during a session; lists options for enhancing the productivity of the middle of a meeting.
0-7863-0429-4   178 pages

INSPIRING COMMITMENT

How to Win Employee Loyalty in Chaotic Times

Anthony Mendes

Shows how companies can gain the trust, loyalty, and commitment of the work force, even during times of heightened flux, while improving performance through effective goal maintenance, decision making, and team-building.
0-7863-0422-7   125 pages